The Family Celebrant

&

Officiant

Ceremony Guide

du bureau du droit d'auteur
1179410

2021 COPYRIGHT ®

The Family Celebrant & Officiant

Table of Contents

Page 7 ~ PURPOSE

Chapter One: Introduction

Page 8 ~ What is the Canadian Society Of Celebrants? Being a member of the CSOC

Page 9 ~ Curricula expectation

Page 10 ~ Profile Testing and Certification of Volume Two Pre-course Assessment for Certification and/or Pre-Requisite work for a Diploma?

Page 11 ~ The Prerequisites for a Diploma

Page 12 ~ Mentoring

Page 13 ~ What is a Certified Family Celebrant? What are Celebrants?

Page 14 ~ The Mission

Page 15 ~ When you are the evaluator

Pages 16–18 ~ Ceremony/ Tradition, what is the value?

Pages 18–26 ~ Contingency Planning/Ceremony Cancellations

Pages 26/7 ~ Is a Bespoke Ceremony a Hybrid ?

Page 28 ~ Secular and Non-Secular/Metaphysical(Spiritual) Ministries, Pastoral And Ceremony Services

Page 29 ~ What really is the Family Experience ?

Pages 30-5 ~ Leadership And Public Speaking

Ceremony Guide   CSOC

Table of Contents

Chapter One: ==Introduction==

Page 36 ~ What is a Family Celebrant ?

Page 37 ~ The Anatomy Of Ceremony

Page 38 ~ What is a Ceremony ?

Page 39 ~ What to expect in the following chapters

Chapter Two: Betrothal/Commitment Ceremony

Pages 39-41 ~ Selecting a package from the booth /The Price List's coverage

Pages 42-44 ~ The handfasting tradition And Unity hand-wrapping(An aspiring modifying guide)

Pages 45-8 ~ The Interview Checklist And Questionnaire

Page 49 ~ The Standard Handfasting Ceremony package's: "Mock Invoice" to sample

Pages 50-55 ~ Handfasting Ceremony Script/Client Copy

Page 56 ~ The Sales Receipt

Page 57 ~ The Commemorative Certificate Keepsake

Page 58 ~ The Package Modality

Pages 59-60 ~ Hand Wrapping/Handfasting Ceremony Initial Interview/ Ceremony Draft

Pages 61/9 ~ Gay Ceremony Commitment (2ndDraft)Script

The Family Celebrant & Officiant

Table of Contents

Chapter Two: Betrothal/Commitment Ceremony

Page 70 ~ Anatomy of A Ceremony

Chapter Three: Child Naming/Blessing Ceremony
Pages 71-115 ~ Presentation Folder/
~ The final interview and practice/
~ Order Of A Ceremony sample/
Pages 72-104 ~ Nathan's Naming Ceremony
Pages 74-86 ~ Child Naming Ceremony Sample Draft/
Celebrant Script copy
Pages 87-89 ~ Anatomy of A Ceremony Sample
Page 90 ~ Naming Day Certificate Keepsake Sample
Pages 91-92 ~ INVOICE And PRICE LIST Package Sample
Pages 93-106 ~ Questionnaire/Interview Checklist
Pages 107/10 ~ Naming's/Blessings/Order & Structure/outline
Pages 110/15 ~ Religious & secular readings for
child naming/blessing ceremonies
Efficient & Effective

Chapter Four: Nuptials And The Undoing &
Parting of Ways Ceremony

Pages 116/20 ~ What are the Celebrant's Responsibilities
Here In Canada ?

Page 121 ~ "THE ROLE OF CEREMONY"
(defining who we are; by knowing what we are not).

Pages 122/3 ~ Atheist/Humanist and Civil Celebrants/
What a Humanist Order of Ceremony might look like

Page 124 ~ A Wedding Menu/Price list, to Sample

Pages 125/37 ~ A client ceremony package

Ceremony Guide   CSOC

Table of Contents

Chapter Four: Nuptials And The Undoing &
                Parting of Ways Ceremony

Pages 138/40 ~ What are my Options? Packages and Pricing

Pages 141/43 ~ What is a consultation?

Pages 141/46 ~ Some adaptable Script pointers & Content Order

Pages 147/48 ~ Anatomy of A Ceremony for Bethany And Janine

Pages 149/67 ~ Celebrant's Copy of a Wedding Ceremony Draft

Page 168 ~ What are Conjugal Relationships?
           Things a Celebrant cannot say nor do.

Pages 169/71 ~ A Nuptial in Wicca, is called "Handfasting".

Page 172 ~ "Scripted Toast"(before/after wedding)sample

Pages 173/4 ~ Non-Religious, Optional Poems & Readings

Page 175 ~ Religious: Corinthians 13:1-8;13(modified excerpt)
           A Non-Religious Reading, for a Break Up

Pages 176/80 ~ About the "Parting of Ways Ceremony"
               (how to undo from the previous Nuptial sample)

Pages 181/2 ~ ODYSSEAN WICCAN CEREMONIAL sample
              Set UP & TOOLS

Pages 183/6 ~ Describing the Odyssean coven's handparting
              & parting of ways, Wiccan ceremony sequence.

Pages 187/8 ~ TO SUMMARIZE/THE TAKE AWAY

The Family Celebrant & Officiant

Table of Contents

Chapter Four: Nuptials And The Undoing & Parting of Ways Ceremony

Pages 189/93 ~ Ritual tools/ Altar setting/Seals & Sigils

Pages 194/5 ~ Initiations and psychological impacts

Pages 196-201 ~ What A(legal)SEPARATION AGREEMENT might look like.

Pages 202/3 ~ Celebrant boundaries & Canadian Law
~ In Summary

Chapter Five: Renewal of Vows Ceremony

Pages 204-6 ~ PERFECT LOVE & PERFECT TRUST

Pages 207-9 ~ MODIFICATION And ADAPTATION

Pages 207-24 ~ Sample a ceremony package

Pages 225/6 ~ A House Warming Party

Pages 227-38 ~ A Complete copy of a client's script sample

Pages 239-40 ~ The Sales Receipt sample/ Certificate of Vow Renewal keepsake

Page 241 ~ "Renewal of Vows" ~What is it?
~ *A modified take away, from the religious version of Matthew's blessing for a marriage, by the Corinthians 18:20.*

Ceremony Guide   CSOC

Table of Contents

Chapter Six ~ This is It !

Pages 242-45   ~ To recap: Initial Meeting/Interview Checklist
~ What happens after the initial meeting?
~ Approving Ceremony & Transcript Delivery
~ Modification of the Ceremony Script
~ During the Ceremony and After

Pages 246-50   ~ What else is there ?
~ COMING OF AGE/COMING OUT/ A HOUSEWARMING
~ Theme & Culturally Combined Celebrations

Chapter Seven ~ In Closing

Pages 251-6   ~ Advertising/Having A Social Media Presence
~ Society Vs. Association
~ Some Common Questions
~ The Questionnaire

Chapter 8 ~ WHERE DO WE GO FROM HERE ?

Pages 257-9   ~ Practical Evaluation&Examination Sheet

* NOTE:

* Although not a mandatory prerequisite, as the hardcover print.

Also made AVAILABLE IN E-BOOK FORMAT

ISBN: 9781777104139

The Family Celebrant & Officiant

PURPOSE

Constructive practices for Celebrancy and Officiating.

A family guide for ceremony involvement and modern rites.

This book and for each chapter made specific, the following;

<u>Agenda</u>:

Betrothal/Commitment Ceremony

Child Naming/Blessing Ceremony

Nuptials And The Undoing & Parting of Ways Ceremony

Renewal of Vows Ceremony

This text, is designed as a continuing reference; it can be an excellent source for public relations and a valuable gain, from the realization of its importance. Canadian Society Of Celebrants motto: is to bring together the "<u>B.E.S.T.</u>" forward !

    Business

    Education

    Spirituality

    Training

<u>NOTE</u>:

  This book is a series, from VOLUME ONE

    ISBN 9781999017095

  The Funeral Officiant & Ceremony:
  A Course In Funeral Celebrancy

Chapter ONE

What is the Canadian Society Of Celebrants?

<u>The vision</u>: A collaboration with other like minded entrepreneurs to form a mentoring incentive from the educational CSOC. To build and provide programs that can bring about more Celebrants and Ceremony Officiants.

<u>The mission</u>: To provide a curriculum through self study books; such as this one and an online presence, that can assist in certifiable courses toward a diploma.
The purpose, is to help build a like minded society and an online membership, for Canadian Celebrant training; with theoretical and a mentorship practical component.

Being a member of the CSOC:

Canadian Society Of Celebrants, is not a licensing providing body; as of yet there has been no regulated requirements in place for Celebrants to carry a licence.
The CSOC is a legal corporate entity and should the need arise for such standards to be in place; it will aspire the CSOC and its members by offering this option. Upon certification from the CSOC the initiation into the CSOC begins.
You can then become a member and for a yearly fee be kept on file as an active. As members the aim is to bring education with business by to training and hiring. A healthy record keeping and reporting incentive is our mission(as per pending qualifications); that on occasion from this list will be asked to mentor and/or perform such said qualified duties.
There is no stipulation however; that states a member of such standing cannot be ordained, as a minister or have any pastoral affiliations (as well as licensing) outside of CSOC.

All are welcomed inclusively to join in...

The Family Celebrant & Officiant

<u>Curricula expectation:</u>

Welcome to the last and final installment. This book will be a necessary curriculum; toward a diploma; however on its own exclusively is geared toward A Family Celebrant Certification. The curricula does start the reader on an independent study path from volume one, and stands as a timeless potential for many other probabilities to be made possible. A diploma can be obtained through either requirements of "Volume One" and in the same way as with "Volume Two"; they do not necessarily have to be in that order of; however both certifications are required in order to obtain a diploma. Online tutoring feedback and a one, on one mentoring can take place, however optional. Feedback on assessed work is only optional for portal members and further advice to better guide improving on performance. An online course will also give this book for an opportunity and/or just directly through electronic feedback; for written commentaries and individual discussions. These options are the tools that will be made use of via e-mail/or on line project(s); quiz(s) and finally a certification. This book is the hard copy; however any other correspondence can be made upon proper payment to request further learning: of your own completed script and payment per assessment script. This designed structure is to help accommodate for those who might not be able to invest the time and/or money right away and/or all at once. Whether you approach it from a Volume One and/or Volume Two, with interest firstly; know that both roads will eventually lead to the same destination for a diploma, if you so wish it. As things continuously unfold for us; it is an ongoing process that will require from our own life path destiny.
As the reader wishes to progress and from their own authentic timetable.

By purchase of this book your enrolment has commenced.

Profile Testing and Certification

Yes it is true that most insecurities can easily be alleviated with criminal background checks. A lot of associations and that does include potential employers, do obsess with psychological testing and criminal background checks. The Celebrant profession, is normally not that interesting to those young and fresh out of high school. Celebrants are normally those people interested at the stage of their lives and where they have already experienced enough to know themselves. The younger the age group it must be well addressed to psychologically compartmentalize accordingly for better mentoring and basic militant effort training be applicable. Canadian Society Of Celebrants, is an advanced level of training and academia.
For those who are not sure just exactly where they stand in all of this; than perhaps entrepreneurship is not for you. More appropriately a career directions program and profile testing boot camp might just be the very thing. Canadian Society Of Celebrants, is driven by an interdependent component; to build a fellowship that thrives naturally and by this stance, to resonate with a mature entrepreneurial spirit. Volume Two Pre-course Assessment for Certification and/or Pre-Requisite work for a Diploma?

After successfully completing the reading of this book the next step would be for certification and/or obtaining a diploma.
In both cases a copy of the book's assigned "Pre-course Assessment", as proof of having purchased a hard copy of "Volume One" (this book) and have completed reading it; along with a 500 word biography of yourself, with a most recent quality photograph must be sent via email with the subject title "Family Tutorial". You will then be contacted with an invoice to be made out to the Canadian Society Of Celebrants, either via PayPal and/or e-transfer.

The Family Celebrant & Officiant
The Prerequisites for a Diploma

* You will be expected to come up with a 500 word biography of yourself and have a quality photograph(of yourself).
On the diploma, a quick response generating system code is added; along with the Canadian Society Of Celebrants official seal. This will ensure to sustain the legitimacy of you, as a paid member annually. Upon receipt of the diploma and including all certified documents (that we ensure for all our stay-on members); Canadian Society Of Celebrants, fellowship's profile blog/web page and all other social media directories. Please ensure your biography indicates and what it is that you can do, for your future/clients?

> This will be your first Family Celebrant tutorial assignment; it must be emailed and along with all the other prerequisite requirements, for approve. Should this be the first book you pick up to read; then the same will apply upon payment to this course certification. For more clarification and further inquiry contact canadiansocietyofcelebrantss@gmail.com

Step 1: email the following to the above email address.
> Your name as you prefer to have it show on the certification and your place of residence address for proper mailing of an authenticated sealed and approved by the CSOC. Please include a telephone contact number; email and/or media webcam name.
> * You will be asked for a copy of a ceremony script; this will be of a ceremony you perform(ceremony script will be modified, that your clients identities can be protected).
> * You must video tape the performance and as a rehearsal run, prior to the actual ceremony; submit along with the above script, for further feed back on your practice and monitoring quality.

Mentee/Coaching:

A qualified person that can help to oversee and by showing up, for your first ceremony. Should the location be unreachable, other options can be made available; such as via webcam. The educational program, is as lively and interesting as we choose to make of it. To get proper feedback on your practice; the experience that will help build your confidence and add clientele as well. It is a prerequisite for a diploma; however other arrangements can be made adaptable and open to negotiate a fee, for an actual CSOC member...to encourage each protégé, is well prepared and appropriate to fulfill the project objectives. Knowledgeable speakers and evaluators; that have been through the same course of experience. Evaluations are a means, through which we can all benefit, to improve our leadership skills; as well as, public speaking and overall performances. This is a team effort, from which we can all learn and continuously expand our growth together.
As the reader further continues to explore, for a diploma; every member of Canadian Society Of Celebrants, must know how to evaluate effectively. We(for those feeling ready) must further explore to grasp, and utilize in this volume. After the diploma the protégé member will be capable (if not after this family certification); to explore these possibilities and from having a few ceremony try outs under their belt, already. Members must be encouraged to speak up and exhibit a level of leadership; that otherwise, might never be accredited, anywhere else. Positive reinforcement, raises the bar on self confidence and is a crucial step to help achieve new goals and recognition. Mentors can recommend more practice; give pointers, on where the speaking and performance can improve; by giving specific examples (in complete privacy to make positive suggestions).

The Family Celebrant & Officiant

What is a Certified Family Celebrant?

Trained and certified, to provide a meaningful stress free ceremony. Throughout our lives we methodically go through some very important occasions and that we must mark down in our calendar. From the moment of birth we can recall each year to celebrate and with it all the many special relationships we forge along the way with others. In the past religious officials were the only recognizable formal officiants; they could accommodate as well as help us manage to bring about these services.

From traditionally standard practices to highly personalized events and as imaginative as the creative palette can accept to offer. Thanks to the "Family Celebrant", ceremonies can now be spiritually designed to reflect the personality, lifestyle and beliefs of the person and/or family that wish to celebrate.

We are here to encourage participation by family and friends to also co-create into a meaningful event. We are responsible in writing the script for the entirety of the performance and assist with the facilitating process to direct and guide the ceremony along from beginning to the end. From the falling in love commitment ceremonies and other such occasions; to the difference between an actual legal matrimony of marriage and a wedding celebration ceremony; to baby blessings/baptisms and so on as we read along…Some of the more traditional concepts will be emphasized and given chapters from which to train the reader with.

What are Celebrants?

Focused individuals and/or a grouping of practicing ceremony professionals (in some cases hold council for licensing) with a common intent of bringing folk together, for a special occasion. <u>Ceremony Officiants</u>: are passionate writers/speakers; with their advice and direction, a space can be held for praise worthy events to empower. They are independent contractors, that create from their own schedule.

Ceremony Guide   CSOC

The Mission:
Flexible speaking and adaptive thinking; to expand from what has already been taught, by this volume 2.

It must be exciting and challenging the reader to want to experience. Giving a prepared speech provides an excellent opportunity, to practice your communication and leadership skills; including planning, organizing and time management.

<u>Your evaluator will be grading you on things like:</u>

Speech ability and public speaking; what is your speech introduction going to be like? Your choice of words and audience responses (if any)? How well the script transitions with the flow as sequenced? The overall length and the relevance of the script, style of elemental choices to ritual.

Have you arrived early to check the microphone, lighting and any other props for setting up? In these kind of ceremonies, there will not always be a lectern made available and/or even necessary. Perhaps you can bring your own stand for example; it will reflect well on your ambitious initiatives.

Your evaluator must be provided with all the necessary sheets required for the evaluation and/or proof of book.

Specific ideas that you could apply in future to help better strengthen your content or working with a coach on speech delivery techniques. Mentors are respectfully there to focus on your skills and accomplishments; rather than your personal attributes. Level of competency and speech delivery.

What is your behaviour like and skills when performing.

Only the essential written section of the evaluation from the book is required; however further encouragement and praise might be provided whilst the moment of congratulating from your evaluator.

The Family Celebrant & Officiant

When you are the evaluator:

When you as a member, get called to perform such a duty; it is a great opportunity to practice your leadership skills.
How well do you listen ? _____ Are you just watching and hearing or actually understanding the Celebrant?
Put on your critical thinking cap to give some feedback; but not just that, how motivated did this ceremony make you feel?
Be honest and do not be afraid to give the student some supportive feedback of your own. What was the overall performance of their presentation and leadership accomplishments? Make certain to identify from the pathways of evaluation just where the speaking was successful and where it could more room for continued growth and improvement.
For each presenter that you evaluate collect the data from the few things they did well and mention them; this will help them be more confident the next time around. The goal, is to help all celebrants become upstanding members; that will reflect well, on the rest of our society and future mentees/evaluators.
To become more effective and able to achieve, where exactly our leadership skills can be enhanced and improved toward that result. Where is it, that the student can level up, with their mannerisms and habit forming skills, as well as attitude.
Finally go ahead, review these project objectives and from their book's manual. One of the most effective ways for members to gain valuable feedback on their speaking and overall performance skills, is to record their presentation. Your mentor, by playing back your demo; will be able to further evaluate the effectiveness: of your speaking, hand gestures, poise, eye contact, speed of delivery, enunciation and pitch. These recordings can be made relevant for rehearsals and also, during the actual ceremony. Replaying portions of the recording, during the evaluation of each speakers performance and/or to view them privately, at their own discretion.

Ceremony/ Tradition, what is the value?

Ceremony, is a kind of self expression and as an abstract modification; what we upscale to offer, we must inform on its value. Unlike the traditional well known ways of having things done and performing under certain requirements.

We must explain our practices and ceremonial elements that bring our services to the forefront. The "Unity Traditions" that we incorporate, is one sure way to capture interest.

We start from the familiar ritual formulas and ceremonial elements; then expand from there, to inspire the imagination of our clients further. How is it, that from what we impart to inform and for any special occasion; otherwise our prices will reflect the devalued uninformed expectations.

When assessing the value of something; we must consider the demand of the service and/or product we are offering (Demand Vs. value ratio). We must inform and educate for any service and/or product(s) to create the value; otherwise we will be forced to compromise our prices. This can be very tough at first, when we are starting out; because others who have started just like us, have undermined the value well across the board. Getting people to like us and prefer our business over any other, does have its compromises and pricing should not be one of them. When we are providing a service we must consider our competitors value; Why not respect them as the many aspects of ourselves that come together and in the making for its demand. The quality will not undermine the quantity as we were trained to believe; rather the devaluing and compromising of our standards will. Desperate times require patients to self preserve behind the scenes and by working on oneself so to improve the quality of what we offer. Persevere through this process and your progress will offer to show business value more than what the price is. Stand firm and steady, as you consistently watch carefully, from the boring options in competition.

The Family Celebrant & Officiant

Ceremony/ Tradition, what is the value?

You are not better than them and they are not better than you; the reality of what is showing up is in actual fact not in the showing off. We are not clones nor peers; we all have something authentic, to bring forth and for others (such as ourselves) to appreciate. This is our society in the making and we must support and promote; rather than undermine because of other associations that have lowballed us into client referral.

Through divide and conquer everyone loses; including those who place us on demand to value our services.

Service+Value=Demand.

No one will ever know "The how much we must charge and how much we are worth"; until it becomes a demand.

The future of our spirituality has very little to do with ceremony; however some of us who still love the beauty of ceremony and value the fading from traditions, in exchange to form, from newer ideologies. The preferred standard and social values might not be for everyone and where tradition is over glorified; its redundancy has no place in motivating us; rather it can be replacing the beauty of expression with energetic drain for duty. In preferring to do things in a certain way is not wrong and yet again not even necessary. Monumental increments of time; suspended from their moment and to mark for their occasion. These are the very things we celebrate and from these cycles hold the value for their anniversary and other so called meanings. These things that we can hold most precious and dear to our hearts content.

As we become more in tune and aligned with ourselves and these cycles; the need for doing things a certain way diminish. From the break down and dissolving of what was valued, as tradition becomes more of a legal and religious standard; the ceremony starts to lose its spiritual value. This is where spirituality and creativity has less and less to do with, ceremony and more to do with ideology.

Ceremony/ Tradition, what is the value?

Spirit is progressive when it can express creatively and each moment is valued in this way. As we tune in (with ourselves and each other), to a spiritual understanding; it is not beyond us, nor outside of us. It is not as unreachable to express, from ourselves and how we feel. It is our civil right and not a duty; the need to love and feel within our consciousness; this beauty, is spirituality unencumbered. Ceremony was meant and in this way to be valued. Your script must thrive on originality, giving purpose to the many topics and a clear direction, for the ceremony. After selecting the theme, list as many topics, as possible. Which of them will have the greatest of interest for your client and family. Coordinate with them this theme and program of plans; they have already prepared and offer ways that they can participate, as well as speak.

What is the occasion and who or what is the reasoning for this celebration? The theme must be specific.

Contingency Planning/Ceremony Cancellations

Whether it be an outdoor occasion needing to move indoors and/or the other way around. The location and the venue might not be able for some unbeknownst reason; especially when there is a pandemic in our midst. This is something to consider, when dealing with troubled times across the world. What must we do with longer upcoming events, such as weddings and whether or not to postpone or cancel?

Where venues and vendors might be putting plans in place, when looking to postpone. No one wants to put their ceremony on hold; however being flexible enough and for making re-adjustments can make a huge difference.

Such as, in the case of a "Corona Virus/Covid-19", decisions must be made in order to adjust and modify so to adapt; as venues too they must shut down for safety reasons.

The Family Celebrant & Officiant
Contingency Planning/Ceremony Cancellations

Although no one has been through a pandemic and/or a situation of such magnitude before. Each and every day might be revolving with its guidelines and that might impose with its restrictions. Perhaps rules must be in place to limit the amount of guests; as well as how and where the ceremony can or cannot take place. When dealing with municipal, provincial and federal restrictions that are in place regarding bans on events and travel.

The health and safety of our communities must be the top priority for all venues and vendors alike. Why are couples in such a rush and that they would be willing to compromise their ceremony for their planner and vendors alike? Please note that just because your clients are in a great urgency to limit their choices; does not require the celebrant to compromise theirs?

In most cases they were only looking for the legalization and which has absolutely nothing to do with us. In the same way clients prefer the celebrant over the religious official; this can become an "up-or-tuned-in" moment to recalibrate.

More than likely, the family will return; to ask for the most elaborate celebration and in this case a renewal of vows and/or actual unifying ceremony. To consider the very minimal and basic ceremony packages to offer in these cases, is to become mean spirited. We are not just in it for the money, nor can we do any real justice in legalizing at best a marriage.

As religious officials, they too must look out for their parish and question their family's motives (in the form of ongoing life time counseling). Baby blessings might also be a little too uneasy to take place however; because of the level of personal space required and from the point of view, toward a vulnerable infant.

More will be discussed under this chapter's title.

Ultimately, it all rests on our packaging and what we can offer.

Contingency Planning/Ceremony Cancellations

Perhaps the naming of a child, might require a celebrant with a louder and more pronounced voice; or rather a microphone, for those who are to speak and from a distance.
How well can our voices carry and when is it alright, to uncover from our facemasks?
Rather than become mean spirited with one another, now more than any other time before; we are prompted to use our imagination and innovating capacities. Be encouraging, patient and supportive with all families. How about replacing the facemasks with matching handkerchiefs?
Maybe have the brides; maid of honour and bridesmaids replace wearing gloves for a beautiful matching set of long opera gloves and for the bride up to the elbow ? _____
But what about the ring exchange ?
As mentioned before, more will be uncovered under another chapter to reveal and for more unity ceremony options.
The bride may be forced to buy off the rack in order to have a dress in time. The same modifications can be suggested, for bridesmaid dresses and wedding gowns. Why not go casual with a common theme and/or traditionally passed down garments? As for the groom and groom's men; why not replace "P.P.E." gloves, with white pallbearer cotton gloves?
This way no pens; paperwork and/or anything else, that we might come to handle, will not require disinfecting(including our hands). As for the flower vendors; most florists require at least 30 to 60 days to be able to cancel any flower orders placed.
When considering for any vendors and when having to pay for certain materials or costs that have already been acquired. Perhaps they can all be considerably replaced by a last minute shopping at the dollar tree store.

"BE CREATIVE"

The Family Celebrant & Officiant
Contingency Planning/Ceremony Cancellations

Thrift stores can provide for already made bride's bouquet; Or for the materials to make your own. For example, the dollar store can make for a great last minute vendor; to come up for all your frills and ceremonial props. We are not wedding planners, for this read perhaps, is suggested and from the many Martha Stewart books; that she has written on this very subject.

"Keep it Simple, Stupid" might be great for business.
When spirituality, is compromised in value for business however; it narrows the mind, through its limiting perspective and agendas, into the art of boring. From corrupted advertising agency endorsements and with only but weddings to offer, as a prime example. As the push and pull continues, the restrictions placed on religious centres, such as churches closing down.
Perhaps from an authority figure's perspective, the path was always paved with good intentions. As a celebrant; however the path has yet to be fully paved and understood.
Thereby the appearance of the misunderstood circumstances. Where distorted versions of the light, might cast a silhouette of limited opportunities, we watch. From the many officials, who aspire from profiting fame and do not care for a growing parish; rather the risk that they might bring and to their entire ministry, excites them. As a society we are here to help provide the misguided celebrities; as well as the misfortunate celebrant leaders of our time. When we are showing the way for creativity, we are not endorsing in anyway, for its artistic limitations; that creates competition.

"BE VERSATILE BUT NOT MEAN SPIRITED"

Contingency Planning/Ceremony Cancellations

In such said cases and where, many are doing their best to be flexible beyond the terms of their contract; not everyone is pushed into a mean spirited agenda. Before booking for any commercial vendors, advise your clients to always research out their vendor's policy; in terms of postponement.
It is in their own best interest to know what the venues/vendors, might or might not be providing; what these options are and with the proceedings, on a case-by-case basis might be?
When families can go out of their comfort zone, for such extravagance; our part too, must reflect in equal value.
Should the ceremony be compromised and to creatively imagine the elaborate event; that is to take place, than we are allowing our spirits to be compromised. It is not a mean gesture to consider, what our spirits can deflect and to tolerate performing otherwise.

Ceremonies are most popular when the weather can accommodate an outdoor venue; however in most cases even these outdoor venues come at a price. In Ontario all the city parks and gardens must be pre-booked at an hourly rate of $192.01 + HST. The hours permitted are as limited, and in some cases (if not more) than the indoor venues.
The amount of guests can vary on the particular location; that ranges anywhere from 20(Music Garden) people to cap limit of 100(Ash bridge's Bay). Obviously some venues such as in the case of Toronto Island; the availability is much more limited and harder reaching than the others. Some friends and family might have been known to have acres from their very own estate and especially somewhere much nicer than the public venues/vendors.

The Family Celebrant & Officiant
Contingency Planning/Ceremony Cancellations

Suggest your clients to ask around and most often the owners might be pensioners; during these tough times, we could all use that little extra bit of cash flow as an incentive.

Also by changing the popular Saturday ceremony to a Thursday and/or from a Sunday to a Wednesday; this increases the chances for an available venue.

Why not research and by looking up, all these venues; the other options and that are off the Crown's radar, can be made most useful. Off the grid or private property and with the permission of the owner; it can be as simple as your own back yard?
Allow for "AUTHENTICITY"

"With IMAGINATION Anything is Possible" !

Why not have a baby naming/renewal of vows/engagement and/or wedding ceremony in your own back yard?
As a Celebrant you are an independent entrepreneur; we are not piggy backing from any licensing authority and/or nonprofit organization(to hide behind). It is never easy establishing clients, in an honest, for profit way and the lack of support that comes with it. Forming a society of responsible entrepreneurs, is exactly what Canadian Society Of Celebrants, is aiming for and in their members well supporting character.

Prepare your patrons in a way of all the possibilities for having to replace a vendor or two. Go over with them and in such cases these contingencies; of having to postpone for another place and time perhaps?_____What will be their first step to consider?

Always make certain the transparency for any contract; of the fine print and before having them agreeing to it.
Also, how reachable and approachable are you?

Contingency Planning/Ceremony Cancellations

How quickly can you respond to your clients needs?
Are you on the same agreed upon level of awareness and that would also have included in the making of this ceremony, to collaborate with other venues/vendors?

Do your clients understand all the options available and the parameters of each option, whether that be postponing or cancelling? A well informed client will not reflect poorly for any given ceremony that we assign ourselves for.

These are very important details that a celebrant must be given, in the event of a postponement and/or cancellation.

Making certain that you are also compensated in the preparation of a ceremony and for any or all the work that you have provided. As a vendor, do you have a cancellation fee in your packages? What can clients expect in regards to monetary compensation(if any)? What are some of their other vendors within this collaborative venture doing to help?
Do they have an action plan in place?

Are they as supportive in this collaboration as you might prefer, to be willing; and/or to stand by your clients, who need to make these difficult decisions? How are you dealing with the deposits/payments ? Are the other vendors as flexible, to transfer for another location, day and time slot ?

Your clients, might to consider, administrative fees and associated with, making these adjustments.

In circumstances, where a vendor, is not available and for the new date; each client must address this issue, directly with their individual vendors. Some might even be willing to make exemptions to their contract terms and policies.

Contingency Planning/Ceremony Cancellations

Couples also need to understand that if the cancellation has taken place within a very short timeframe, they may face penalties for items that have been ordered and paid for by their vendors. Suggest to your clients before committing to confirm before booking and or ordering from a vendor; this way the client will know. For example: many florists need to confirm their flower orders 4–6 weeks before the wedding date, and once that order is placed. With this given information the client will know when to commit to paying for these materials. Inform them that we as any other vendors will administer a cancellation fee of _____.

Inform them of these administration duties that will include us as celebrants that we must charge in the same way that any other vendor/venue deposits would for holding that date and/or any other materials and inventory for that particular client/date.

No venue or vendor wants for their clients to be affected over the decision of the postponement or cancellation of their event's celebration. When a catastrophe occurs and with little to no time to prepare for, how is it that we can all co-creatively collaborate with planners and vendors as well as venues alike?

The more information that is imparted to us and for the ability to share collectively these resources the more secure our clients will be in us as celebrants. We as celebrants must motivate a level of flexibility to impart our potential clients and enthusiastically with them; that they too can learn to be flexible in their expectations.

Ceremony Guide   CSOC

Contingency Planning/Ceremony Cancellations

Imagination can transcend beyond the disappointment for a certain image to uphold and on the value standards for celebrant to officiate the ceremony. The clients might be looking for a public figure and that they might not get their first choice. A celebrant is not a celebrity by any means.
As celebrants we must not compromise integrity and/or our confidence in our capabilities; because of these well meaningful misunderstood distortions. As the Covid restrictions continue to set us back from our many achievements to say the least; we will find way of adapting. Social distancing; masks, gloves and various other postponements heading our way, such as lock downs.

Establishing private portals and with live personal interactions that we are connecting to one another; for the most part, have kept us thriving and with each member's consent for these types of viewing. We have gone "Hybrid" and in every sense of the way imaginable; as nothing is, as it used to be.

Is a Bespoke Ceremony a Hybrid ?

It has been said somewhere before that "variety is the spice of life". It is from the previous ideas to blend, mix and match with have always been at the apex of popularity. Unfathomable this controversy that finds us, in discrepancy; to explore and at what capacity we can find acceptable. Elaborate and made applicable only for the "Crème de La Crème".
This pristine magnitude, where did it come from;to trickle down, in its custom made, (convincing us) through evolution and to bestow amongst us, as traditional?
Within every creative passage is held in by an inner vision called "FAITH".

Is a Bespoke Ceremony a Hybrid ?

From one culture to the next we have formed tribes; that resonate in unifying the custom made and holding it down, into the blending of religion. What might have been a perfectly aligned feeling to express, so long ago, inherited and legitimate; might feel awkward, irrelevant and most importantly (fake)now, as just going through the motion. <u>Interfaith is not the same as having faith in all the possibilities from infinite potential</u>.

Forming a different perspective on the familiar, is the key ingredient, in creating a bespoke ceremony and script; it is derived directly from an artistic and solution oriented mind. In this case a hybrid ceremony is birthed from a bespoke ceremony.

A bespoke ceremony in its testimony, also had to have come from somewhere? A completely original ceremony and within its configuration, is inconceivable however; because it too, is in a category of variables to denote. Although the script's modality can be considered as bespoke; it again falls into place, within the hybrid structures, of its confines. When something is trendy it becomes "viral"; this is how bespoke turns into hybrid and vice versa. The template can be altered and within this hybrid method the blanks that require filling in, is its custom made sequence. When we modify something we alter the custom, to some conceivable degree and/or other. Whether it be from synthetic and/or completely original ideas; to personalize a ceremony is to bespoke it. The hybrid method is best described as a synthetic creation and interfaith connected. A bespoke ceremony, is a co-creative design, focused on creative and collaborative expressed intent; to experience and from a place of <u>having faith, in all the possibilities, of one's own infinite potential.</u> This topic can also be found in the first novel and in its level of contraction; for some to be better understood when limited. In some cases, such as marriage, the law of the land, always takes precedence and will be further discussed, in chapter four.

Secular and Non-Secular:

Non-traditional in that "Faith" forms religion and not the other way around; in this way we can go deeper to find our client's personal philosophy and from which to "Bespoke a Ceremony".

The Canadian Society Of Celebrants, is thereby an organization that can better be identified to group and promote such dedicated souls; be they Agnostic and even Humanistic-Atheist, all paths are welcomed. Although Celebrants might walk the same path of spiritual philosophy as their religious counter parts and that would include some metaphysical and spiritual alliances; by no means is the Canadian Society Of Celebrants, in any kind of legally administered and/or religiously affiliated binds.

Metaphysical (Spiritual) Ministries, Pastoral And Ceremony Services:

The metaphysical and spiritual parishes, are legalized entities and like any other religious ministry; however not limited to interfaith complexities. Nor is the ceremony that it officiates, in this way subject to be under the Christian and/or any other hierarchy collaboration. Adhering to all the laws of nature, it can organize, as well as alchemize in all energetic equations; into something that will benefit its focus of intention on and in service to the greater good . The Celebrant does and can have many peers, it can look up to; for the purpose of pastoral collaborative, co-creation and this most definitely can include such ministries. Including and for all denominations of priesthood/pastoral brother and sisterhood alike affiliations.

The Family Celebrant & Officiant

What really is the Family Experience ?

The family experience, is all about bonding to further expanding relations and grow as a community. All their requests, as the Celebration will revolve around the coming together and in bonding with whatever theme will create to expand these values of family, friends and intimate relations uniquely to identify with and shared. From its ancestral communications passed along to the grieving survivors for interpretation and the ability to satisfy this connection. It is about finding just the right frequency with that familiar channel and through best fitting, a reconnect again. Anything less of its vibration just won't do. The need for cultural identity has us promoting into certain tribes that can support us. This concept, is made reference to and sometimes it could be viewed, as a paradox, when mentioning "traditional".

For some it is the only cause for celebration and for others the agitation to reconfigure just the same; however it does have its level of importance to value. Respect through knowledge of these collective agreements is a moral and ethical common courtesy. We all must start learning from somewhere and in this case synthetic ideas are easier to grasp than in their original raw state. Like any other invention, traditions take the lead in most of the adolescent training for a truly remarkable celebrant.
Be open to the unknown, it is not a deviance; rather the unknowable experience of ceremony, can and will better define you as brilliant as you are the "guide". Know that everything always starts off as a preference and in most cases with tradition.

Leadership And Public Speaking ?

Public speaking has been taken to another level; as has, our marketing strategies. A global pandemic has created for us, to innovate and unto another platform, of social media.
Whilst Skype is being archived; other social media platforms are showing up and to take us to yet another level, of public speaking. Facebook/U-tube webinars continue to take centre stage; other messenger providers too, like LinkedIn and Zoom, do provide the podcasts and online networking systems.
Speaking directly to a person can have its techniques to sample the pace and speed of our tone of voice. What are some of the topics that others can interactively engage to respond ?
Present your thoughts concisely and effectively; to encourage group discussion and debate. Allow for flexibility and adaptive speaking from these online discussions. The more flexibility, the more quality will be brought forth by the unexpected responses of our audience. In this case of honing into our calling as celebrants; we will not be concentrating to that extent and of where it does not concern us. By leveraging these strategies, normally the overall ambience for the speaker; must be connected through the magnetism, of common ground and mirroring capabilities, to match for likeability.
An online presence is not the same, as a live human interaction and where we can make use of the space; but do not become to invasive. As the numbers grow in audience from the one or two persons we are speaking to; the approach of the presentation must then again, be modified. Maybe we can recover, to coming out again and as we had done before.
Whilst keeping this in mind; find the few, that you can find to focus on and that best describes your audience, that you are speaking to. As the crowd gets larger, the common ground for the gathering must be the focus.

Leadership And Public Speaking ?

Great public speaking, is heartfelt and creates a connection with your audience. But how do we find the way to capture our audiences interest? After finding out your target audience, then a trust must be built. A heartfelt speech, is excellent; however just remember, that you are not there to perform, as a motivational speaker and that you can read, directly from your script.
Although a familiar appearance can do wonders for the ambience; it really has no olfactory hold on the web's social media.
Your voice however; is the new magnetism and over any other appearances. Eye contact, can also become more forgiving and where otherwise the guests too might have connected; during the key points of your script. The tone of your voice and how you choose your words cannot only move mountains; but also cast spells(in a good sense of its meaning). Be expressive and sincere. Remember you are now up closer and with a microphone; relax your voice into it. Don't waste the connection that you have going already, with superficial ice breakers either. Rather best to pause during the most relevant moments and wait for others to respond; or at the very least to absorb and ground what has been said already. This will create a powerful impact and just before the mind chatter is to start up again, then pounce with warmth and confidence.

These tools are not to be taken for granted; must be mastered well and with the confidence of your own self esteem to back it up.

This inner knowing of the lion's heart, to voice throughout the jungle and be heard by many. Tenacity builds trust and integrity; do you have the discipline to achieve alignment to this inner passion and to share it well with others?

Leadership And Public Speaking ?

Never rely on the external comparisons to build your confidence with; the support must be generated from your self esteem and that is an inside job. There are many different types of public speaking: Strictly from the mind and memorized as to reverberate. With great practice the script can be re-enacted brilliantly. What a huge difference it can make to have it coming from the heart; rather than executed strictly from just by reading directly from a script. Just speaking from the heart and expressing from the moment; can be scrutinizing and subject to others conflicting beliefs. The combining of the mindful, well rehearsed script and until it does become believable, is the secret.
Plan->Practice; Rehearse and Execute.

Whether it be reading from a script; or triggered Q-cards and/or Power-point incentives, it must be well structured and connected. Some people love to write; while others prefer to read out loud and some are equally loving both.
When you make the choices of where to put your energy, effort and passion; do you do it for your own integrity, circumstance and awareness of yourself ? Can you support, commit and be loyal to what you honour and believe in; (not to undermine others) to show the world who you are, what you care about, think and to let them know where you will bend but never break? A good leader must be who they are and realize that they can live up to their own potential. Dare to dream the best version of yourself that only you can be and support others to do the same? Be in the pulse of things. Everything must get along within the rhythm and flow in synchronizing synergy. While rehearsing and creating your script, a timer and/or stop watch is essential.

Leadership And Public Speaking ?

The timer/stop-watch, will give the added pace to your speech, performance and practical adherence, to a time frame.
A timed well script is our responsibility and to fulfill this role for the many others we must know each presenter's speech to average out and confirm for the actual length of the ceremony.

The hallmark of effective speakers, is the ability to express themselves and within a specific amount of time.

Are you someone who can speak from your truth, set boundaries, trust your instincts, follow your heart, and advocate for yourself ?
Sail on this excitement and not the crippling fear of the many questions or the doubts and those what if's that might arise.
Place your bet on the real of this voice and the words coming out and do not allow the fear of what isn't devour the very same notion of public speaking and as excitement would for its intent.
Leadership requires that a person has a directive and more than likely a few steps ahead on the audiences primary interest.
The strategy is in the planning and that comes from an "Anatomy" and that of the order of its many probable causes leading to the one prediction of intent, you are the driver that will see us through the ride as passengers. Public speaking without a script requires some kind of key-points of power and that will support.
As well as, to keep you from losing track, or focus, from your audience's distractions and that could otherwise throw us off our game. The order of events the script must follow and who is responsible for what, can be found on the "Anatomy of Ceremony" template. As the Officiant you are the leader of the Ceremony.
Confirm the time allotted for each prepared speech, from the speakers and other responsibilities of participants.

Leadership And Public Speaking ?

The sequence of events are explained in the clearest way possible for your "<u>Anatomy of Ceremony</u>" template. All is timely recorded and each participants name and/or group; ceremonial elements and rites of passage in synchronized order. This will be the skeletal version of the ceremony sequence. This is where a template of the skeletal view, called the "<u>Anatomy of the Ceremony</u>" can come in very useful. The "<u>Anatomy of the Ceremony</u>", is our version of the Q-cards and/or power-point precursors used wisely in a public lecture and/or speaking. The "<u>Anatomy of the Ceremony</u>", is made exclusively by the Celebrant who will be Officiating as a guide. Knowing when who will be coming online and who will be taking a back seat and what must be in cue as the segments unfold in perfect timing. For every Ceremony Script the secret component is this skeletal template and as we progress further into reading we will come across the "<u>Anatomy of a Ceremony</u>" attached to every Celebrant ceremony draft.

Your ability to organize your thoughts quickly and respond to impromptu questions is not so much the case; rather a well prepared speech and for the other speakers that we must officiate the chance. With "<u>Family Celebrancy</u>" the orchestration of the choreography is more to do with than just the public speaking. We are not revolving around the celebration of a loved one who has passed away this time around. There will be more participation and involvement around a couple or a baby that the rest of the participants will have a say and/or role to play. Introduce yourself and briefly state the purpose of this gathering; keep your remarks brief and enthusiastic. Once you have prepared the script check for the following: Does your speech have an effective opening, closing, and primary points in the body of your speech?

The Family Celebrant & Officiant
Leadership And Public Speaking ?

You may choose to memorize your opening and or closing as well as other essentials normally presented to confirm and make official. Consider the transition from one segment to the next; does your script shift smoothly and flow well into each other. Just like our thoughts, actions and words, must act like bridges; so too, the elements that come together, must connect to best support the ceremony and all the events that tie it together.
A well organized script will link together in a cohesive way, to ensure your content is supported. Maybe it's time to start acting and believing; in that today, is that day and start taking action. So can you stand strong and appreciate your own unique gifts, talents and beliefs; whilst still being able to appreciate others, and support their magnificence, without jealousy or judgment? Do you have the empathy and compassion for yourself; to acknowledge the well deserving praise, from time to time and nurture yourself, where others have never been able to?
An opening technique that grabs your audience's attention and puts them on the edge of their seat; Tell a story that covers some pivotal moments that bring us closer to connecting with the family units experience; What most resonates with this gathering by getting a feel when playing around with the theme and in connection with the emotion you wish to capture out from their reactions(sad/cry-laugh/happy). Hold their attention through out the transitions; by stimulating them seamlessly, into the next elements of the ceremony and then closing, into a motivational high, from it all.

What is a Family Celebrant ?

With exception to Quebec(www.etatcivil.gouv.qc.ca).
In Canada, an Officiant does not have to be a licenced religious official; nor a certified celebrant with a diploma even.
Families can prefer to have their event led by someone more familiar. Firstly the value is more apparent in its scripting service. Secondly, in officiating and thirdly, in public speaking. This is where your prices for extended consultation and professional services, might require some discerning and in what order they be valued. The creative process is encouraged for the family and those who are just starting out; to form these kind of bonds with others. When couples and groups alike, can be given the encouragement to co-create and express in any way, shape or form. We are here, as guides to make suggestions and assist in the direction of the ceremony's process. Whilst keeping in mind that, although we can collaborate with our patrons plans, to help and further give advise, for all their special ceremony provisions; we are not the event planning makers. As Celebrants, we must be prepared to give the right kind of relevance and officiate, over a diverse range of unforeseen circumstances expected and/or unexpected; wanted and unwanted life events. From the marking of a divorce; to a personal retirement occasion that can include readings, poetry, music, songs, the giving of a toast and other interactive games and meaningful activities. Don't retreat just yet, this book can help to motivate along your development.
Just know the more you keep at it, your script writing style, it will evolve; along with your officiating and placement into, for almost any conceivable event. Perhaps a launching of a new club or any other business venture to commemorate and celebrate the ties, we have with others. A "Family Celebrant", is a well respected and functional occupation; bringing humanity one step closer toward enhancement and dignified relations, with each other.

The Family Celebrant & Officiant

The Anatomy Of Ceremony

Just like any other special event, a plan must be set in place. Much like a rehearsal, a skeletal structure is designed and as a walk through the entire ceremony. In many instances and where a rehearsal is not possible; a walk through is more private, less formal and highly recommended. All participants must know their place and what will be expected from them, prior to the ceremony. As the Officiant, you are there, to orchestrate and guide the ceremony. The anatomy of ceremony, is the complete outline; from opening, to the body and then closing, to conclude. It is a road map, to the first step of determining your destination and plotting your route. An effective way to prepare your script objectives; it gives purpose to the many points, you wish to talk about. A transparent overview of the gathering's main event and detailed expectations; into a logical sequence, that will help achieve this goal. The subjects of ritual and props involved; that revolve around the main point, for the ceremony.

Naturally these topics will be the focal point of description and how it makes this ceremony relevant. There are many variations to structure in a template; eventually you will come to find your own adaptation and to create with, for this purpose.

Although improvising without a script is not a good recommendation, this is how it can be slotted in.

A template designed(even for the unexpected and unscripted surprises) for whom so ever wishes to conduct the ceremony. Exclusively designed to walk the Celebrant through each and every step, of who is doing what and when. The anatomy allows for(interactions of the flow and rhythm heartfelt moments), the Celebrant to be timely aligned and from within this structure; as it unfolds collaboratively in flow. After the initial meeting and interview checklist; a skeletal structure will secure your ceremony plans and confidence as an Officiant.

What is a Ceremony?

An organized ceremony will help immensely for your clients to formulate their thoughts and ideas from the opening line right through your closing statement. All of the components must link together and be motivated by the families personal needs and not by others(just remember this).. Analyze how you can encourage your clients expectations from your point of view and how you can better understand exactly what they wish for, from you...The opening of your ceremony is designed to motivate the interest and level of excitement for its relevance.
Why are we gathered here today?

Your outline will include all of these expectations; from the body, it must work its way and like a climax, right through to closing. The conclusion, is the climax and all the other segments in between, must be threaded in together, from the start. To summarize the entire ceremony; you might choose to begin, as well as end it, with a powerful story, quotation or illustration of your primary purpose.

These services can be basic, to most elaborate creative expressions, of nature and in ritual design; inclusively and exclusively, for society and the individual. It will evoke the theosophical reflection, traditional life and personality affiliations, of those we serve.

For the purpose of this volume, the focus is on Family and revolves exclusively around that kind of story for creating.
In this case the reader can become empowered by its awareness and perhaps carry onto its connective course, that will provide certification... More importantly, the know how from this book; that will deliver to the reader and much more confidence, to participate in this kind of practice....

The Family Celebrant & Officiant

What to expect in the following chapters:

Mock ceremony drafts from start to finish and script to sample. Optional take away variations of reading/ritual formulas and ceremonial elements; to play around with their stories.
From traditional to hybrid and bespoke; aspiring the way, on how to adapt and modify their templates. Your potential client is shopping around and wants more information on your prices. Think of your price list as your cover letter and your package as the resume. Unlike the traditional and cultural religious officials we are not; therefore we must create our value for the consumer. Perhaps they see us advertised on "Yelp" or any other "google" and social media endorsement agencies. Our web site might only show a price list and/or just a cover synapses of what we offer. Perhaps they visited our blog or any other social media advertisements. Now that everything is mostly done on line it makes it so much more efficient. Rather than physically taking the time to visit them in person and/or webcam consultations.
Why not simply start with emailing them your price list; a further explanation of your package; an Interview Checklist and with it an invoice. The next thing logically is the payment and the consultation if at all necessary. Be always open for any kind of communication; whether it be initially by text, than a phone call and/or a live and interactive webcam conference, with the family.

Chapter Two ~ Betrothal/Commitment Ceremony

All ceremonies tend to gravitate around the essence of a theme and well grounded symbology within ritual(s). It is through the element of ritual and that can best describe, the impact a ceremony can have; to imprint from a believable and well executed, practical relevance and to mark for any occasion. Putting together a package for each and every ceremony, will become the familiar take away; throughout the many chapters of this book. It is highly advisable and not just from a marketing perspective; for all practicing Celebrants, to grow accustomed to.

Chapter Two ~ Betrothal/Commitment Ceremony

The following package will utilize a Celtic unity ceremony, with a hand-fastening element. There are so many others to choose from and depending on the culture: for example an exchange of rings can suffice; then to be later enhanced, following the matrimonial nuptials. For this chosen sample's purpose; it is to fully explore and take apart. With the idea, that it can again be put back together, by the reader; to adapt, re-authenticate and recreate packages, for your very own, future patrons.

The Family Celebrant & Officiant

Peerless Moments
" BESPOKE YOUR CEREMONY "

Handfastings, Commitment Ceremonies; Renewals and Baby Naming

CEREMONY   PACKAGES:

Starting Fee

The initial 50% payment is **$169.**⁵⁰

"The Engagement"
Handfasting Ceremony   **$ 339**

The handfasting knot that is tied is a symbolic representation of oneness between the couple and can make for a beautiful event to show the unity, of becoming bound to each other. **This is a "Commitment Ceremony" and can be made to accommodate for any other Unity Traditions!**

- Initial Consultation/Ceremony package
- Unlimited telephone meetings and online consultations
- (optional) A keepsake copy of Ceremony script/short rehearsal (optional)
- Officiate Ceremony (any day of the week)
- A signed proof of keepsake certificate(Witnessers~2)

declare the intent to enter into this union, the hands of the couple are clasped and fastened together with a cord or cords just before, just after, or during their vows are made to one another. The wrapping of the cord forms an infinity symbol.

. **TRAVEL EXPENSES ~**
Anything over a 30km range is subject to an additional $2/km consideration.

- NB: 50% Initial Deposit Fee is Payable before starting and with a 25% Non- Refundable.
- Final Agreed Invoice to be paid in full on the day of Ceremony and before the paperwork signing.

© 2019 Canadian Society of Celebrants   1

Ceremony Guide   CSOC

"BESPOKE YOUR CEREMONY"

Q. Do you have to be Wiccan to have a handfasting?

A. No. In fact, the term *handfasting* arose during the early Christian era, when Paganism had already lost much ground. It's the symbolism that Wiccans and other neo-Pagans have reclaimed and today embrace. The betrothals eventually became so formal that it was an event in and of itself, which eventually lead up to the wedding ceremony. People from all religious denominations can experience the beautiful handfasting ritual during their Wedding/Renewal of Vows ceremony and/or as the Engagement to commit to one another (for a year and a day). In practice, Wiccans are taught to place well-thought intention into ritual, and therefore they do so into the knotting of the cords. There can be many variations of the traditional handfasting. After the bride and groom both declare their intent to enter into this union, the hands of the couple are clasped and fastened together just before, just after, or during their vows are made to one another. The wrapping of the cord forms an infinity symbol. The handfasting knot that is tied is a symbolic representation of oneness between the couple. In a show of unity, they become bound to each other.

The ritual of the handfasting invites a unique, creatively magical experience between the couple. But you don't have to be Wiccan to feel the magic if your intentions are true. Also, the ceremony does not have to follow in that particular religious order and can be expressed as creatively and alternatively as you desire.

Q. "What is the best material for Handfasting?"

A. Some people prefer ribbons, for delicacy, while other couples prefer cords, for symbolic strength. You decide? The length is normally about a yard long, or a little less as in a meter, and for a three-cord hand-wrapping, coloured cords are often braided. To weave beads or other objects in, you might want to use a smaller diameter cord.

Ribbons
Have the widest range of solid colours or ribbons with patterns(hearts) ?

The Family Celebrant & Officiant

" BESPOKE YOUR CEREMONY "

"Hand-wrapping"

The colour, length, type and of number of cords used to handfast is entirely up to you. Some suggestions can be as follows: 1) while facing each other, the couple placed their right hands together and then their left hands together to form infinity symbol while a cord is tied around their hands in a knot. 2) Couple can choose to either a) hold hands and cord/ribbon is wrapped around wrists in a figure 8 type fashion-the infinity symbol-or b) they hold elbows, (Groom right to Bride left), and then bind over the forearm lose enough for them to drop into holding hands for the kiss as the cords make the figure 8 around their wrists, then make a comfortable exit. 3) Another way is that the man and woman place their right hands only together while a cord is used to tie a knot around their wrists. 4) You may want to face each other and have the binding of both pairs of your hands(Two-handed fastenings constituted as a fully legal marriage throughout Europe whether the blessing of the church was sought or not).
5) Another way is to have only the right hands, and another one of each right and left. There are many variations of the handfasting rite. Again it all depends on your preference and how you might perceive its meaning might be similar to the way you where your rings(engagement/marriage).

Guests:

You might like to invite others in to tie; wrap around and or just simply hold and carry ribbons, and would be most of help to us when officiating.(Please ask your guests should they decide to bring ribbons that we must know a head of time and that they must be about a yard long Note* these details must be added in the questionnaire and/or the Checklist provided within this package).

Again it is entirely up to your discernment to whether or not; this ceremony entails gently wrapping cords around the bride and groom's clasped hands and tying a knot, symbolically binding the couple together in their declaration of unity. The fastening materials can range from colours and have whatever meaning attached to them as you may want to make believe and closer with what most resonates with you. The material can range from traditional cord to a combination (with other trinketry that can be attached to) or simple laced colour ribbons, from: silk to satin and as simple as you wish; to most elaborate and depends entirely up to you.

© 2019 Canadian Society of Celebrants   3

"BESPOKE YOUR CEREMONY"

The following are some of the meanings attached to the handfasting colours:

Red - will, love, strength, fertility, courage, health, vigour, passion

Orange - encouragement, adaptability, stimulation, attraction, plenty, kindness.

YELLOW - ATTRACTION, CHARM, CONFIDENCE, BALANCE, HARMONY

Green - fertility, luck, prosperity, nurturing, beauty, health, love

Blue - for a safe journey, longevity, strength, tranquillity, understanding, patience, health

Purple - healing, health, strength, power, progress

Black - strength, empowerment, wisdom/vision, success, pure love

White - spiritual purity, truth, peace, serenity and devotion

Grey - balance, neutrality, used in erasing, cancelling, neutralizing.

Pink - love, unity, honour, truth, romance, happiness

Brown - for healing, skills, talent, nurturing, home & hearth, the earth

Silver - for creativity, inspiration, vision, protection.

Gold - for unity, longevity, prosperity, strength

This package is all about "The act of handfasting" and as originally it had intended; an element to a formal betrothal ceremony (the precursor to today's engagement) perhaps going as far back as ancient Celtic Scotland, up to the 16th century reformation-era. During the formal betrothal ceremony, the agreement (a trial marriage) was a formal handshake to seal the deal in future marriage and the pledge by the giving of the hand.

The cords are not permanent but perishable as a reminder that all things of the material eventually return to the earth, unlike the bond and the connection that is love which is eternals. For this reason:

We simply prefer as close to ancient Celtic; in that 3 cords/ribbons to place
Red/Burgundy, to symbolize romance, partnership and happiness.
Ivory/White, for peace, sincerity and devotion, and gold.
The theme is simplicity and with it our many ribbon roles of satin otherwise it starts to escalate in price and really this particular type of service to commit with at its origin from hence it began; was never intended to be costly.

The Family Celebrant & Officiant

" *BESPOKE YOUR CEREMONY* "

The theme is simplicity and with it our many ribbon roles of satin otherwise it starts to escalate in price and really this particular type of service to commit with at its origin from hence it began; was never intended to be costly.

The Following Interview Checklist and Questionnaire pretty much can help to further organize for your selection and further expand from the above information that was imparted for you.

Ceremony- Interview Checklist

CONTACT DETAILS

Client 1 _____ (Preferred Name)

Client 2 _____ (Preferred Name)

Address _____ 2nd Address _____

Email _____ 2nd Email: _____

Phone #'s Phone #'s

CEREMONY FOR:

Full Name _____ fiancée / fiancé

DOB: _____ Where?: _____

Full Name _____ fiancée / fiancé

DOB: _____ Where?: _____

© 2019 Canadian Society of Celebrants   5

Ceremony Guide   CSOC

BESPOKE YOUR CEREMONY

Ceremony- Interview Checklist

How many guests: Do you want them to participate with the holding and placing?

PARTICIPATING FRIENDS & RELATIVES:		
	Client 1	**Client 2**
Mothers Fathers Brothers Sisters Children Cousins Friends		
Other/: 2-Witnesses(option) YES / NO To sign w/proof of keepsake certificate by us.		
Venue: **Time & date ?:** **Location?:** **Accessibility?:** **Contingency?:**		

The Family Celebrant & Officiant

" BESPOKE YOUR CEREMONY "

==Here's a handy list of questions to help get you started:==

==*keep in mind that this ceremony has a duration commonly topping 15-20min. anything over can affect price to range.==

How long have you known each other and why have you decided to commit?	Fiancé: Fiancée:
What colour, length, width, material type and number of cords/ribbons? Will you be providing them or do you prefer our standard simplicity and preference to colour?	
The Binding What style would you like; ex. From 1-through-5 and/or just leave it to us to formulate the way: YES / NO ? (if you circle NO please be descriptive)	
About your betrothal? YES / NO 1)**Personalized Vows** to recite before and/or during; written by either or both partners? _____ Do you prefer us to at an extra cost? Yes / No Note: no more than 2½ minutes be given and for each recital of these promises to each other. ("will you marry me" & as simple as the proposal)	Fiancé: Fiancée:
The standard recital can be formatted with each ribbon/cord before tying the knot and can be worded in any preference that you wish to give meaning for each colour that will bind you together (for 366 days and/or until the matrimony). PLEASE DESCRIBE: Or do you prefer it left to us ?	
What is your favourite colour ? Do your choices come up with a secondary colour you might like to also use	Fiancé: Fiancée:

© 2019 Canadian Society of Celebrants   7

Ceremony Guide   CSOC

Peerless  Moments

" BESPOKE YOUR CEREMONY "

<mark>handy list of questions to get started</mark>:

What did you think when you first saw your fiancé / fiancée? (Both must answer)	^Fiancé: Fiancée:
When did you realize you were in love? When did you first say, "I love you?"	Fiancé: Fiancée:
What was your proposal like and who proposed?	Fiancé: Fiancée:
What words did you recite when proposing?	Fiancé: Fiancée:
What do you most respect about your partner?	Fiancé: Fiancée:
How has your life gotten better since meeting your mate?	Fiancé: Fiancée:
What about them inspires you?	Fiancé: Fiancée:
Anything else ?	

The Family Celebrant & Officiant

INVOICE #007

PEERLESS MOMENT'S
" BESPOKE YOUR CEREMONY "

officiant@msn.com
467-716-4673

DATE: March 07, 2018

BILL TO

NAME / George Flowers
ADDRESS 20 Brenda Crescent
Toronto ON. L23 4TZ
georgef@msn.com
PHONE: 416 979-2319

FOR

The Commitment
/Handfasting Ceremony

Details	AMOUNT
(standard) Handfasting Ceremony	$339.00

Initial Consultation/Ceremony package
Unlimited telephone meetings and online consultations
short rehearsal

1-Signing of commemorative certificate

	SUBTOTAL	$339.00
	TAX RATE	0.00%
	OTHER	$0.00
	TOTAL	$339.00

THANK YOU FOR YOUR BUSINESS!

Ceremony Guide   CSOC

" BESPOKE YOUR CEREMONY "

Sample of Client Copy

HANDFASTING CELEBRATION

FOR

GEORGE FLOWERS & HEATHER EARL

Tuesday, March 27th, 2018

5pm
Allan Gardens

19 Horticultural Ave, Toronto,
ON N5A 2P2 Ph.No. (416)392-7288

© 2018 Canadian Society of Celebrants   1

The Family Celebrant & Officiant

" BESPOKE YOUR CEREMONY "

Officiant arrives at 4:40 pm
Meet & Greet
Administrative/set up

Officiate/Rev. gives a little intro.

Good afternoon and welcome so wonderful that you have come to participate with this occasion. My name is _ _ . _ . . . . and I am here like all of you to help facilitate in this here Ceremony and as the Officiate. This is a nice straight-forward ceremony with all the key elements.

Heather Earl and George Flowers have invited us here today for an ancient Celtic Tradition called the "Hand Fasting Ceremony"

If there is anyone present who has just cause why this couple should not be united let them please hold their peace until the final marriage day!!

We are here to give recognition to the worth and beauty of love,

To add our best wishes and blessings to the words that make for this engagement so special. It is out of the routine of ordinary life that we come to hold a sacred space open for George and Heather.

They are in love and it is never too late to hold hands,

To remember to always say I love you every day does not constitute for a great marriage and with the right person; rather it is being the right partner.

Ceremony Guide   CSOC

" BESPOKE YOUR CEREMONY "

If the couple has written vows they wish to speak to one another, now is the time to do this.

Officiate/Rev. George and Heather can you please come together in front of me and face each other please.

All are holding hands now and have connected in a circle around the couple.

George Flowers Vows: As I stand before you, looking into your eyes,
I see all of the things I fell in love with.
As I stand here before you, my heart beating so strongly,
I find myself so lost for the right words to say.
As I stand here before you, just like on that one fine day with ring in hand and you said "yes" I asked you to marry me; must have remembered because you are still wearing it " and here we are not so many days later making it official that we are engaged.
It makes me remember too something and that is just how complete you make me feel. It makes me remember every laugh we've shared and every beautiful moment there is to come.
Here we are today in the presence of so many others that we are blessed with to amplify the love we share and with their support to participate and make stronger this ceremony.
With this tying of the knot, my heart my soul; I give you everything I am today, to hold and cherish every moment.
I promise to love you, protect you, be with you forever and let it be known I chose you. Let it be known, that with this ring that you have accepted and are now wearing, I promise to be with you for all eternity, 'til death do us part.

© 2018 Canadian Society of Celebrants   3

The Family Celebrant & Officiant

Heather Earl Vows: I stand before you and proud to wear this ring
And in shame that I did not give you one just yet to wear.
Proud to have felt like this and
ashamed to not have enough words.
To explain exactly how I feel
And let everyone know at instance but I'll try.
Not through words right now
But in showing you and for the rest of our lives;
Well, I guess we will have to see how it goes,
How long it will last and how far this will take us.
What love had done to me, God only knows
And how this love has led me here
To stand right next to you
"Happy".
And I'll do whatever I can
To make you feel just as "Happy".
As I am having you in my life
And I can't wait to do so.

Officiate/Rev. The vows of love have been spoken.
I ask you now to cross your hands over each other,
and take one another's hands.

© 2018 Canadian Society of Celebrants   4

Ceremony Guide   CSOC

" BESPOKE YOUR CEREMONY "

Rev./Celebrant

We will now do the ancient Celtic hand fastening ritual where 3 cords will be placed over their joined hands.

Robert 1 will now place the Burgundy cord to symbolize romance, partnership and happiness.

Evette 2 will now place the Ivory cord which stands for peace, sincerity and devotion.

Greg 3 will now place the gold cord which represents unity, prosperity and longevity.

Anna 4 will now tie the cords together to signify the tying of the knot.

Rev./Celebrant

May the vows you have spoken never grow bitter in your mouths.
As any child discovers when they are learning to tie their own shoes,
the first move is to cross the ends.
The cross creates the (X), which is the symbol of partnership and union.
As your hands are bound by this cord, so is your partnership held by the symbol of this knot.
As this knot is tied, so are your lives now bound together.

Woven into this cord, into its very fibers, are all the hopes of thy friends and family, and of themselves, for a new life together.

With the fashioning of this knot you tie all the desires, dreams, love, and happiness wished here in this place to your lives for as long as love shall last.

© 2018 Canadian Society of Celebrants   5

The Family Celebrant & Officiant

Rev./Celebrant

In the joining of hands and the fastening of a knot, so are your lives now bound, one to another.

By this cord you are thus now and forevermore bound to your vow.

May this knot remain tied for as long as love shall last.

May this cord draw your hands together in love, never to be used in anger.

The two of you now entwined in love, bound by commitment and fear, sadness and joy, by hardship and victory, anger and reconciliation, all of which brings strength to this union.
Hold tight to one another through both good times and bad, and watch as your strength grows.
I shall now remove the cords.

Rev./Celebrant

Heather and George, this cord ribbons symbolizes so much.
It is your life, your love, and the eternal connection that the two of you have found with one another. The ties of this hand fasting are not formed by these ribbons, or even by the knots connecting them.
They are formed instead by your vows, by your pledge, your souls, and your two hearts, now bound together as one.

As one last bond, you must kiss now!

May the happiness you share today be with you always.

It has been my honor to officiate your ceremony today.

Thank you !

• Parchment Signing with Music

Total time roughly __15__ minutes

© 2018 Canadian Society of Celebrants

Ceremony Guide CSOC

SALES RECEIPT

BESPOKE YOUR CEREMONY

officiant@msn.com
Toronto
467-716-4673
maria@peerlessmoments.com

RECEIPT NO. 007
DATE March 7, 2018
CUSTOMER ID PM007

George Flowers
20 Brenda Crescent
Toronto ON. L23 4TZ
georgef@msn.com
416 979-2319

PAYMENT METHOD	Bank/e-transfers	Credit Card

QTY	Package #	DESCRIPTION	FULL AMOUNT	AMOUNT PAID
1.00	(standard)	Handfasting Ceremony	$ 339.00	
				$ 84.75

	SUBTOTAL	
	TOTAL	$ 339.00
		(84.75)
	OWING $	254.25

Please pay the remaining balance in full by the day of Service !
THANK YOU FOR YOUR BUSINESS!

The Family Celebrant & Officiant
One-signing of a Commemorative Certificate Keepsake

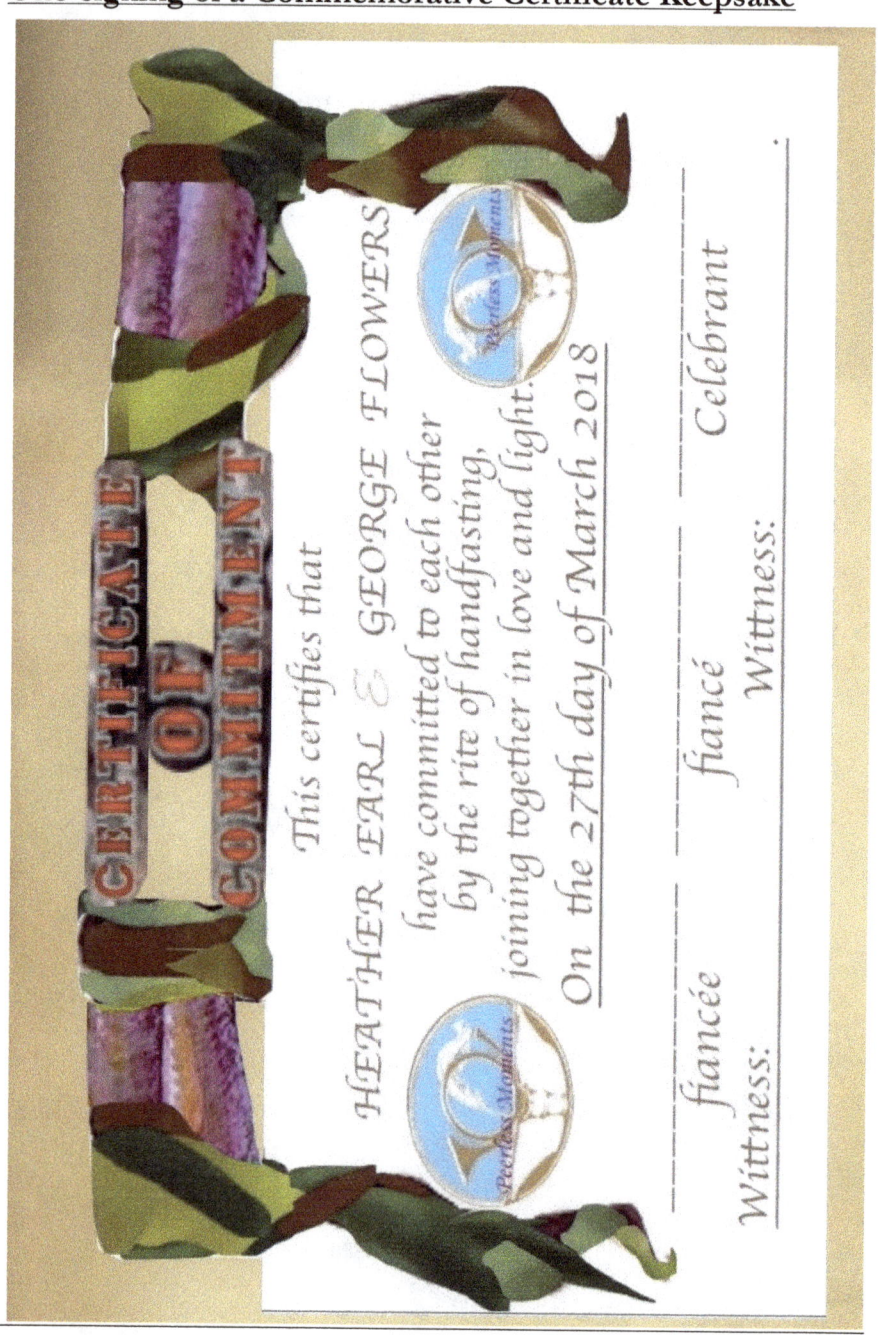

Chapter Two ~ Betrothal/Commitment Ceremony

The Package Modality:

As every package, ultimately must have a pricelist.
In many cases there is more than one package on a price list. After a package is selected, it is accompanied with an invoice. The invoice can be stated all the particulars, and as such a partial or full payment must follow. The package normally expands from the pricelist; in depth and on the substance given for the ceremony. Attached to this package is a handy list of questions; to help along with the interview checklist and then followed by the invoice. When the payment deposit is applied; then the booking, can solidify. Whether partial and/or the entire amount is paid in full, a receipt can follow. It is entirely up to you and how you wish to run your business, to add in the taxes(depending on your province); some might wave it as a discount and/or simply include the taxes in, as a flat rate concept.

In this case it is a commitment Ceremony. The purpose of the commitment ceremony, is to make a public declaration of a life-long commitment, love, and dedication between two people.
A commitment ceremony can be held at any time, wherever your client wishes.

A commitment ceremony, is also taken in its interpretation to mean the engagement. Not too long ago same-sex couples were not allowed the privilege to be married; a commitment ceremony was very popular and in this way somewhat distinctly different from an engagement. The commitment ceremony by any other means of passage is the same thing as the traditional engagement. In this case and depending on the culture, a ceremony does take place. Unity ceremonies and their ceremonial rites of passage; will be further discussed and expanded on, as we continue along. It can be anything from the exchange of rings to the following given sample of this package.

Hand Wrapping / Handfasting Ceremony

Those of you who have been to a Greek Orthodox ceremony, will undoubtedly recognize the symbolic binding of the hands; at the end of the service and that stimulated into the idea "Bonds of Holy Matrimony". During the middle ages rings were for the very rich and afterwards became the common custom for engagement practices. It was during the middle ages that holding hands, became popular and as a public sign of exclusiveness. During this time the idea of a simple cord; rather than a ring and that had started from the finger, to the wrist. Some modern and more fashionable jewelry of today have been exhibiting these styles; of a gold ring and with a small fine chain that attaches to one's wrist-chain. Before the 1940's and in lieu of a church wedding, Scotland legally recognized this outdoor ceremony. After the 1930's it became considered, as a commitment ceremony; it lasted for a year and a day, followed by the formal marriage. Wicca recognizes two phases of marriage: betrothal and permanent marriage. Betrothals last for one year, and the couple can secure their bond permanently with a "handfasting" ritual. Traditional interpretations and symbology; are strictly used as guidelines, to sample from: for example, the Wiccan meaning of each ribbon colour; to the many ways of binding and that can be best modified accordingly. For instance the colour variations might be interpreted to have a different attachment for the couple.

What they agree to believe and in how they feel to give meaning; will reflect directly on the script and its performance, for the entire experience. The explanation of each ritual beforehand is not only important in the package, but also within the script to introduce the segment in with its traditional origin and original meaning (of tying the knot). A Celtic tradition where the hands are tied with ribbons; or cloth and in the shape of the infinity symbol.

To symbolize the bringing together of the two (from their pulse on their wrist as one heart beat.)hearts in a marriage of strength and unity forever.

<u>Initial Interview</u> – In the spirit of preparation the Interview Checklist accompanied with the questionnaire, is a designated module within the package. The interview checklist can be modified, to use for all your ceremonies; as they all contain similar and special ceremony elements, to include.

The checklist is an important tool designed to be self explanatory. It must be an integral part of your craft and during this course; whilst learning how to complete properly, becomes the skill. Over time you will have accumulated many examples of poems, prose, readings, vows, to fulfill your clients.

<u>Ceremony Draft</u> – On completion of the initial interview checklist, you will be expected to formulate the first draft of the ceremony and in accordance with your clients' wishes. Research the venue as well as you are able to; maybe you can gain accessibility, to see and get a feel for it, first hand.

Is there an event planner, that you might want to get better acquainted with? _____Assess the pitfalls, or where the shortages might be avoided and in their folly, with your common sense. Seek out the venue crew for guidance and collaborative advise from the event planner. Contingency planning is so very important and as it was covered before; it is also on the Interview Checklist to be discussed these options. It is also wise to check that these negotiations of back-up plan have venue and event planner contractually in agreement. With covid-19 and whatever other reasons, encumber the ceremony. After getting a rough idea of the kind of venue, the ceremony is to take place in and the plans there of; we can start to formulate the anatomy and draft the ceremony. Once an anatomy of the ceremony is formulated and a draft has accumulated; from there, the client must evaluate and critique it. Perhaps an online meeting might work best to thoroughly go over all the bumps and snags.

The Family Celebrant & Officiant

Chapter Two ~ Betrothal/Commitment Ceremony

<u>Ceremony Draft</u> – When the couple is satisfied with the order of the ceremony and the draft; then we can progress to the final sample as shown (pages48to53)and right after the followed by the receipt(pg.54). More will be discussed about this process, of reaching the final draft, final Interview and practice; to progressively continue in Chapter 3. There is a lot of freedom with this kind of unconventional ceremony; in that it is all up to the couple to creatively explore. It is not to be compared with and to go off with anyone elses standards, these scripts are special in their makings as peerless moments. A full on creation of what the couple wants and that can best reflect the relationship with each other(fun/childlike/spontaneous) unconditionally and without any legal contracts; with no legal aspects, we must avoid pronouncing them as married. On the other hand it can make for a very intimate and private commitment unity ceremony before and/or even right after the legal and governing matrimony approval.

It can be so valuable to have a well meaningful script for these personal and spiritual occasions. The option can also be made to have a commitment ceremony for those who cannot legally get married and then if and when they can(depending on the law of the land) the couple to change their last names at a later date.

More will be explained, further in chapter 4.

A Commitment Ceremony, is a very alternative way to celebrate your love with your partner. It is a spiritual bind that breaks free from societal standards and expectations that may imprint as burdens upon the couples everlasting love. The beautiful thing about a "<u>Commitment Ceremony</u>" is that, it can also be interpreted as an engagement; and/or as a ceremony, after the long awaited engagement. There is no real linear way when it comes to the imagination and the creative process, does not have to become so compartmentalized.

Ceremony Guide   CSOC

Chapter Two ~ Betrothal/Commitment Ceremony
A Gay (revised draft) Ceremony Commitment Script

The following is of a revised draft from
A Gay Ceremony Commitment Script

Note: that all names and information have been re-enacted for the couple's privacy To show how super spiritual, meaningful and symbolic a commitment ceremony can be.

<u>Public Announcement:</u>

Good evening everybody. Welcome to Fantasy Farm, and welcome to the commitment ceremony, of Stephen and Adam. All of you look terrific. My name is _____.
I am a celebrant from the Canadian Society of Celebrants.
It is my honour to be officiating this engagement.
The ceremony is about to begin, turn to vibrating mode on all your hand held devices otherwise the volume of the ring tone will indicate just whom we can point the fingers at to blame.

Processional- Of Adam and Stephen
Wedding Processional from "The Sound of Music"

                                              ~2 min. 6 sec.

CELEBRANT

 Please rise to meet our happy couple.
You may be seated, thank you. Welcome

The Family Celebrant & Officiant
Chapter Two ~ Betrothal/Commitment ceremony
A Gay Ceremony Commitment Rough drafting Script

Welcome everybody. We are thrilled that so many of you could make it here today. One of the wonderful things about a ceremony such as this one, is that it also serves as a pre-rehearsal for what is destined and to become a multi-family reunion. I am wowed by your lengths you are willing to travel, to be here and for an event like this; which just goes to show, how important it is, to mark these happy transitions in our lives.
We have guests here today from all over Canada and the United states. Welcome! Adam and Stephen, thank you for traveling here today.

Honour Parents

The engaged couple to be, would like to acknowledge the spiritual presence of some people and who meant a great deal to them. Adam and Stephen are very happy, to finally have the privilege of such a special event and after 5 years of being together; they deeply regret that their parents are not physically here today, to join in this celebration. Stephen never had the opportunity to know Adam's parents, but Adam had the privilege of knowing Stephen's parents, who were so very warm and welcoming from the first time that they met. Although Stephen's father is Jewish by his given name, his Portuguese mother, immediately made him feel like a part of the family; a role which was easy for him to assume, since he grew up in a Portuguese family himself.

Ceremony Guide   CSOC

Chapter Two ~ Betrothal/Commitment ceremony
A Gay Ceremony Commitment Rough drafting Script

READING As per Stephen's and Adam's request; they have asked me to read an excerpt from Plato's Symposium. [I will begin to read now].

PLATO'S SYMPOSIUM EXCERPT

Love is our best friend, our helper, and the healer of the ills that prevent us from being happy. To understand the power of love, we must understand that our original human nature was not like it is now, but different. Human beings had two sets of arms, two sets of legs, and two faces looking in opposite directions.

From these 3 sexes: two men called the children of the sun; two women called the children of the earth, and thirdly, that of a man and a woman, called the children of the moon. Due to the power and might of these original humans, the Gods began to fear that their reign might be threatened. They sought for a way to end the human's insolence without destroying them and Zeus divided them in half. In this way too, we became separated, and with only one overdeveloped side, we are always looking for our other half. Those whose original nature lies with the children of the Sun are men who are drawn to other men, those from the children of the Earth are women who love other women, and those from the children of the moon are men and women drawn to one another. I truly believe that when we do become aware of our other half; unlike any other's reach and out of the other's sight, even for a moment, we feel lost in an amazement of love, friendship and intimacy. Like twin flames, we resonate our lives together, desiring for our souls and bodies to be melted into one; this is the very expression of our ancient need. Perhaps this reasoning, is as biological in tune and as nature had originally intended; as one in complete wholesomeness, with the yearning pursuit, of a complete and connected love.

The Family Celebrant & Officiant

<u>Chapter Two</u> ~ Betrothal/Commitment ceremony
A Gay Ceremony Commitment Rough drafting Script

CELEBRANT:
~It all began when Adam held the door open for Stephen, at the Halloween fundraiser; the Million Dollar Smiles for disadvantaged children. Stephen and Adam do you remember how you felt when you first saw each other, that very moment? Adam, what impressed Stephen the most was that you did not push the button, can you still feel the weight from the automatic door. Stephen, can you remember how it pleased you to see how fast that door had opened for you?
Do the both of you, remember what costumes you had on?
Both of you, can you remember the very sight of each other, the sounds of each other's voices hitting your ears for the first time?
Did you ever dream it would lead to a day like this?
Can you believe it? Your lives unfolding in this way, together.
It's even more joyous, than you could possibly imagine, right here and now !

Please face each other and take each other's hands, so that you may feel the gifts they bring to you. Hold each others hands and feel the strength of love, friendship and commitment.
The passionate caress to cherish and in their comfort, you may rest, for many lifetimes over. Look into each others eyes and feel the connection of this compassion to be the encouragement and through adverse times. As your dreams together they unfold, with the same momentum; in unspoken tenderness from this embrace.

Chapter Two ~ Betrothal/Commitment ceremony
A Gay Ceremony Commitment Rough drafting Script

Adam

Before I met, you I felt incomplete in the wide field of my mind. I did not know you then, we somehow kept on, like two distant shores, destined for each other. Like two figs sharing in the same tree; we were apart, yet connected by every thought as the same seed within us.

Stephen

Through my many circles I did know of you and had a burning desire, to join in with your flame of freedom. Our paths collided and did join in love. Your flame completes my flame and united we become just like the Sun. Our brilliance will shine upon the earth and illuminate the moon; to bless our union, as one and in this, our life's endless circle.

Adam/Stephen Together

My beloved soul mate, you hold the key to the locket of my heart, that opens to blossom in the spring and nurtures endless summers; where the icy hand of winter never touches.
I thank you for your patience. Our joining is like the many schools of fish in deep blue waters frolicking; the ocean that meets up with the sea, the lightning with its thunder, the rain that fills the river banks and even more. We are the peace that reigns across the battlefield with laughter. Together we can rise from the ashes and to hear in each others cries, the words – I love you.

Ring Bearer, please bring us the rings, thank you.

The Family Celebrant & Officiant
Chapter Two ~ Betrothal/Commitment ceremony

The ring blessing:

This wooden bowl before us was made out the flowering Koa tree. It is the second most common amongst the Hawaiian Islands and where you both love vacationing together.
Koa is a treasured and valuable hardwood that represents integrity and strength, which are foundational qualities.
By dipping a Koa wood bowl into a body of water signifies two things: First, washing back into the ocean, symbolically, any hindrance to your relationship. On this table and in this bowel, with pacific salt water, I will dip the Ti leaf and sprinkle three time over the rings while reciting the Hawaiian Ho'oponopono, reconciliation, to re-lease with grace any past relationships, both separate and together, clearing your pathway for Aloha (new beginnings).

Native to the Big Island of Hawaii, the Koa wood and Ti leaf ring blessing has a lovely meaning, and is beautiful in its simplicity. The Ti leaf represents prosperity, health and blessing of body, mind and spirit.

The officiant then begins by taking the leaf and dipping it into the bowl, and the water is sprinkled three times over the rings while the following chant is recited: Ei-Ah Eha-No.
Ka Malohia Oh-Na-Lani. Mea A-Ku A-Pau, (May peace from above rest upon you and remain with you, now and forever).

Then go ahead and exchange rings.

[Stephen], you will go first. Please place [Adam]'s ring on the tip of his ring finger and repeat after me.

Chapter Two ~ Betrothal/Commitment ceremony

Celebrant/Stephen (repeating)

My commitment and love for you is as circular as this ring, with no beginning and no end. It represents what has been and what will always be; a symbol of my love as solid, sturdy and with every caress just as tender. I promise you my unconditional love/and I give you my unwavering trust/when others look at this ring they will know that you belong to me and in faith of this love I have for you always.

You may slide the ring all the way onto his finger Adam, it's your turn.

Celebrant/Adam (repeating)

[Adam], you will go first. Please place [Stephen]'s ring on the tip of his ring finger and repeat after me.

Celebrant/Adam (repeating)

My commitment and love for you is as circular as this ring, with no beginning and no end. It represents what has been and what will always be; a symbol of my love as solid, sturdy and with every caress just as tender. I promise you my unconditional love/and I give you my unwavering trust/when others look at this ring they will know that you belong to me and in faith of this love I have for you always.

You may slide the ring all the way onto his finger Adam.

The Family Celebrant & Officiant

The following prayer is for your commitment to each other and will be recited in Hawaiian and English

Ho'ao Pule (Hawaiian Commitment Prayer)
E ka Haku, e kokua mai ia maua e ho'omana'o i ka manawa a maua i launa mua ai,
Lord, help us to remember the time we first met,
a me ke aloha nui i ulu ai ma waena o maua.
and the strong love that grew between us.
E kokua mai ia maua e ho'ohana i kela aloha
i na mea ma'amau i 'ole e ka'awale
Help us to apply that love in practical things so nothing divides us.
Ke nonoi ha'aha'a nei maua i na hua'olelo 'olu'olu
a piha me ke aloha,
We humbly ask for kind words filled with love,
a no na pu'uwai makaukau mau e noi i ka huikala,
a e huikala aku. and for hearts always ready to ask forgiveness, as well as to forgive.
E ka Haku, ke waiho nei maua i ko maua male'ana i loko
o koa lima. 'Amene.
Lord, we leave our marriage in your hands.
Amen.   (Author unknown)

Pronouncement and Kiss: In the theme of indigenous and legally unauthorized ceremonies. I asked both [Adam] and [Stephen] to sum up their relationship in one sentence.
They both answered: "*unconditional love*".
Tonight is all about the native and primal desire that has brought these two together. The unconditional love and upgrade with compassion. That brings us here to witness their joining and taken to the next level of their journey together; to commit as best friends and companions.
To further seal this deal, of your commitment to each other, please kiss now. ------------------------------------→ Recessional

Ceremony Guide   CSOC

The Anatomy of the Ceremony is exclusively made for the Celebrant, to keep synchronized; it helps to set the order of events(readings, music; followed by some type of activity, then a reception). There is no right/ wrong way to do it. The theme will be appropriate to know and have included in the Ceremony as much as possible to also dress the part if that is required of us.

Anatomy of A Ceremony

Contact: Shmitt family, 50 Pottery Rd (416) 425-9122 Ceremony Type: COM/WED/ROV/NAM
Client(s): Adam Santos & Stephen Shmitt Venue: Fantasy Farm Date: 06/06/18

START

Responsibilities On The Day	Responsibility of Others
Arrive 20min. early to check for (Admin.) everything is in working order and set up Meet & Greet	
Public Announcement	
Please be upstanding	"The Sound of Music"
Cue Processional Music	**Venue / Celebrant TO D.J.**
PBS(Please be seated)-Welcome-Intro	**Music Stopped**
Remembrance Honouring the Parents	
Scene In / Celebrant Reads	
PLATO'S SYMPOSIUM EXCERPT	
Element 1 The Story	
	Couple face each other & hold hands
/ Reader 1	ADAM
Reader 2	STEPHEN
/Reading	At the same time together
Ring blessing	**Ring Bearer Vows Exchange Rings**
Element 2 The story	Ring bearer with string through carries places rings in salt water Koa Bowl
The Hawaiian ring blessing	
Dip the Ti leaf and sprinkle 3 times over the rings whilst words of blessing	
Repeated after Celebrant	**Stephen takes the appropriated ring**
VOWS	says vows and inserts on Adam's finger
	Adam takes the appropriated ring
	says vows and inserts on Stephen's finger
Element 3	
Hawaiian Commitment Prayer	
Read by the Celebrant	
Pronouncement and Kiss	**Cue Recessional Music/ Venue D.J.**
Final words	**Adam and Stephen Kiss**
Thank you's	**move to the dance floor**
Scene Out	
Close	**Reception party begins**

FINISH

© 2018 Canadian Society of Celebrants

The Family Celebrant & Officiant
Chapter Three ~ Child Naming/Blessing Ceremony

<u>Presentation Folder</u>: As it was not mentioned previously; it must be made common practice. At the end of any type of ceremony, to present the clients, with a folder; of the order of the ceremony, ceremony script and any other stationary/sundries, such as, certified signed keepsakes and the wedding program's order of service booklet/leaflet.

<u>The final interview and practice</u>: often takes place within days of the ceremony. Ensure that you fix a date for the final interview and practice and that the clients will arrange for all participants in the ceremony to attend. On rare occasions, the anxiety from the family might come as a surprise; when they ask you to carry out a complete ceremony and order of ceremony re-write. Remember, nothing is as difficult as the first draft and you have already been through most of it already. Just do your best to relieve yourself from any emotional charges and overwhelm, stay calm and cool headed.
You can do this !

Always be prepared for improvisations; because the venue might not always be accessible for a rehearsal and not everyone will easily cooperate, to play along. Connect with the participants and ease their minds, by handing them a copy of the order of ceremony.
The order of the ceremony does somewhat resemble the anatomy of a ceremony template; but it is not. The order of the ceremony is just a highlighted and condensed version and unlike the script's anatomy; the clients will have ordered online and from a stationary outlet. It can alleviate for any panic and perhaps this too, can be a great commodity, to make available for your clients. For further suggestions on the order of the wedding service and ceremony brochures, be sure to research some social media platforms; such as "Pinterest" and other reading materials, (can help to guide you in the right direction). A run through will further accommodate the feedback and suggestions, to relieve for any further alterations.

Chapter Three ~ Child Naming/Blessing Ceremony

Order Of A Ceremony sample:

It can be separate on its own and created be the Celebrant and/or a combination of the entire venue's program and service. In which case the wedding planner, venue or other stationary retailers might have included in their packages.
Your only concern is the ceremony.
The following is a perfect example:

Nathan's Naming Ceremony

* Prelude

* Welcome poem by Officiant

* Intro And Speech

* Tree Planting ritual

* A Jewish prayer Verse 1&2 reading by Henderson grandparents Verse 2&4 reading by Cohen grandparents

*Babylonian Talmud Ta'anit 23a~The Story of the Tree Planter

* The Ribbon inner circle initiation

* Pledging of Parental vows;

* Uncle Jon and Aunt Samantha commit as mentors

* repeated inner circle affirmations

* A group gathering speech blessing

* A poem reading by Edna

* Recessional

The Family Celebrant & Officiant
Chapter Three ~ Child Naming/Blessing Ceremony

When your clients prefer a more intimate ceremony; they will suggest hosting it, at their place. At the house, some arts and crafts innovations can be incorporated. Perhaps creating a simplistic option, with wishing messages and blessings for the child, in a scrapbook; to be made handy for the guests, to write something down. When the child is older, he or she can read the messages.

A good and hardy native tree for the planting can also make do for the ceremony element, to commemorate with.
The Ribbon Ceremony

Is a brilliant concept to play around with and modify to your liking as well. It involves creating a binding circle with child and those who wish to be part of the child's most inner circle.

With due diligence a bespoke, personal and meaningful ceremony can be prepared and ready for its performance. Everything we planned for might not be perfect and just as long as there are no real major catastrophes; the hard work is now behind us and it is time, to press play.
Now let us commence with the Officiating of the Ceremony !

The following ceremony to sample with, has done just that.

Ceremony Guide   CSOC

" BESPOKE YOUR CEREMONY "

Ceremony Officiant's copy:

Child Naming Ceremony Draft

For

Nathan George Henderson

Born on Friday March 18th 2016
To
Edna C. & Reggie HENDERSON

Tuesday March 27th 2018 at 1:30 pm

HENDERSON Family Garden

INSTRUCTIONS   OFFICIANT   READINGS   TIMINGS

The Family Celebrant & Officiant

"BESPOKE YOUR CEREMONY"

Baby Baby Amy Grant 3:55

PAUSE <<<< **You are Home**
When you feel the sunshine on your face
The fresh breeze with every breath a rush
the misty morning's crisp embrace
You are home
Can you hear the Robin's song ?
A new dawn to music and laughter
The budding leaves on the tree
The magical unfolding of each season
The peaceful stream and rushing waters, of the river banks
You are home
Everything you can see and name
your mother's laughter
your father's smile
the love of everyone here
Welcome, **you are home**.

PAUSE <<<< (0.56)

Welcome to this gathering and in preparation for our beautiful boy's naming ceremony. My name is   ; and as a Family Celebrant, I am truly so grateful to be officiating this magical venue.

INSTRUCTIONS   OFFICIANT   READINGS   TIMINGS

Ceremony Guide   CSOC

"BESPOKE YOUR CEREMONY"

PAUSE <<<< A Naming Ceremony gives meaning to a life's path and unique journey of one's earthly existence. For as long as this being wishes and long after to be remembered.

The more people this little ball of light touches will further ripple out his precious existence; to the value in that he will offer of service to humanity. This task to further support; commit; and oversee as responsible adults and mentors for this child. The love we give from here on will be of great influence to see this creature grow as well as the impact we will have on his life. This long lasting impression from us will mould and shape his world; so to further more it will also reflect with admiration, respect and appreciation.

When one day this adult and family man onto him will be the caring wise and knowledgeable. He might even without exception nor promise show up for us the aging.   (1.54)

PAUSE <<< Almost reaching 3 years old, Nathan George, Cohen Henderson was born on February 27th 2013.

He was born at the Henderson General Hospital, where his mother Dr. Edna Cohen worked out of.

On October 25th 2008 a beautiful tall, with curly golden locks of hair had made an impression on her. Reggie RNA (Registered Nurse Assistant) was apprenticing at the time. Edna had become very fond of him, with his rosy red cheeks and flushing face.

3

INSTRUCTIONS   OFFICIANT   READINGS   TIMINGS

The Family Celebrant & Officiant

" BESPOKE YOUR CEREMONY "

Often they would joke around about the Henderson name and his lineage of having any connection to where they worked.

In light humour commentary about the Scottish Henderson and Jewish Cohen as a pair, really owning the hospital. Would get a real chuckle, to how it was and that he got to intern as a nurse, at the Hamilton.
On February 27th 2010, at Reggie's Gulf Club; they made it official and Edna from that day since has been owning up to the name Henderson.

Long after so, ironically enough on their second anniversary and at the hospital for the Henderson's, Nathan was gifted to them.

(1.35)

PAUSE <<<< He came out beaming like a little ball of light; that she had nurtured for 9 months, inside of her. Those 9 months, as she had recalled; many a time was depressing and most frustrating.
It was the hardest thing for her to undergo and battling it out; it came to fruition, from darkness and despair, a light at the end of the tunnel.
He came out without any cry and those blushing cheeks again, just like his father's. A brilliant radiance, from blue to purple and then purest white light; truly as she could recall, a miracle this gift bringer of light.

The whole time the name Nathaniel was to be, the Jewish from his mother's side. George was a given, however the couple had long resisted the idea to name the child after the hospital.

4

INSTRUCTIONS   OFFICIANT   READINGS   TIMINGS

Ceremony Guide   CSOC

"*BESPOKE YOUR CEREMONY*"

The name George had its lineage in Greek and Sumerian time meaning farmer. It actually came from his Scottish great grandpa, who owned much farm land. Being on an island, steeped in lineage of farmer's history they thought why not?

For years Edna & Reggie waited; asking others and giving him more names to see which one he would take on was maddening.

Now more than ever Edna & Reggie felt certain; they no longer needed to confuse the boy. Who was one day called Nathan and the very next George.

Let us commence with the very first element that Edna & Reggie thought to be most appropriate.

(1.50)

1st Element: Tree Planting Ceremony

PAUSE <<<ORDER OF THE TREE PLANTING CEREMONY
We are gathered out here and around this cedar tree, with our boy in center; in the backyard of the Henderson's family garden.
With shovels in hand this tree that is about as tall as our precious boy Nathan George. Our intension here is to plant this here tree in our child's honour and watch the child and the tree grow together.
In this way we are able to celebrate life with life, to involve our child as well as ourselves, to cherish a living reminder of this to mark its importance in our lives.

(1.50)

PAUSE <<< the Custom of Tree Planting ceremony comes from the Jewish tradition.

5

INSTRUCTIONS   OFFICIANT   READINGS   TIMINGS

The Family Celebrant & Officiant

" BESPOKE YOUR CEREMONY "

The *Torah*, is a Tree of Life and as pronounced "*Etz Hayyim* " The belief here is that those who will hold tight this conceptual thought will be forever more happy.

(0.28)

PAUSE <<< In ancient Israel a tree was planted when a child was born—a cedar for a boy, a cypress for a girl. As the children grew up, they cared for their own trees. When they were married, the bridegroom and bride stood under a canopy made of branches cut from the trees that had been planted in their honour years before. Thus, the Jewish tradition formed a strong bond between birth and marriage, and helped.

(0.42)

PAUSE << The story of the Name George and Nathan were previously mentioned. One born from the sky, made offer this gift, from God and from the Earth. As fallen onto her, the brightest of stars; to develop a love for trees and a sensitivity, to the wonders of nature. The child's living history—the roots from which he will grow and the legacy he will carry.

(0.35)

PAUSE <<< Adapted From a Jewish traditional
prayer. Nathan's grandparents instead of shoveling would rather contribute and have requested for instead to have a say from this read. Starting with The Hendersons.

(0.20)

INSTRUCTIONS   **OFFICIANT**   **READINGS**   **TIMINGS**

Ceremony Guide   CSOC

"BESPOKE YOUR CEREMONY"

Greg: **this young tree as our Nathan boy George. Both are unique and original, unlike anything that ever was before or will be. Each began with a single seed, concealing a complex potential that miraculously unfolds with each passing day.** (0.20)

Margaret: Let the roots of this tree forever gain hold and spread deep, drawing nourishment from the fertile earth. So may our child draw nourishment from his own roots—family, heritage. As the tree quickly it sprouts upwards tall and handsome may our grandson grow too. (0.22)

PAUSE : That was lovely thought of and thank you.
    Philip and Phillipa also want to continue with
    the last paragraph of this read. (0.15)

Philip : May the trunk grow healthy and strong, withstanding the harsh forces of nature and able to support its canopy of branches and leaves. So may Nathan possess a healthy body and a strong moral spirit, holding steadfast to his own integrity and withstanding the tempests and temptations that could weaken or deter him. (0.28)

Phillipa : When we will watch these branches bud and blossom, giving shade and beauty for all to enjoy. So, too, may we watch our child bud and blossom to be a blessing and support to family, friends and community, and to make his unique contribution to the world.
Help us nourish and nurture this tree and our child so that they may both mature and prosper on earth.
(0.30)

7

INSTRUCTIONS   OFFICIANT   READINGS   TIMINGS

The Family Celebrant & Officiant

" BESPOKE YOUR CEREMONY "

Final Blessings and Planting

PAUSE <<<< To finalize as we finish off the planting with a blessing; I wish to read an exerpt from the

Babylonian *Talmud* Ta'anit 23a   (0.20)

PAUSE<<<< The Story of the Planter

While walking along a road, a sage saw a man planting a carob tree. He asked him: "How long will it take for this tree to bear fruit?" "Seventy years," replied the man. The sage then asked: "Are you so healthy a man that you expect to live that length of time and eat its fruit?"
The man answered: "I found a fruitful world, because my ancestors planted it for me. Likewise I am planting for my children."

(0.42)

The tree is planted.

2nd[t] Element: The Ribbon Ceremony

PAUSE <<<< While we have come to gather around in a circle what a great idea to introduce with these satin blue ribbons another ceremony. This Ceremony has had its origin from Celtic Handfastings.
As the saying "Tying the knot" for couple's wedding ceremonies.
The concept although similar it has taken off quite well. For those wishing to form a binding circle with child and all others alike who wish to be part of this child's most inner circle. This too will be, where we also combine our promise vows, of responsibility. Whilst at the same time, giving of the name blessing; all within this inner circle of power and for this boy now recognized, we will all agree upon by name to confirm.

8   (1.14)

INSTRUCTIONS   OFFICIANT   READINGS   TIMINGS

Ceremony Guide   CSOC

"*BESPOKE YOUR CEREMONY*"

I take and make ready the suitably coloured/silk ribbon and at one end fasten a loop to fit over the left wrist of the child to be named.

PAUSE <<< Nathan George Henderson this is your NAMING DAY: come forth so I can place this ribbon around your wrist first – bright as a flower and now able to understand and walk to the occasion; Lovely child, we welcome you into our world, into our lives and on this your special naming day, that is made for you.   (0.30)

The ribbon is wrapped around the boy's father Reggie's left wrist.

PAUSE <<< Dad, do you promise to protect and provide for Nathan George so he may grow up to be happy and safe? *I do*   (0.20)

The ribbon is then systematically wrapped around the boy's mother Edna's left wrist.

PAUSE <<< Mom, do you promise to encourage curiosity, courage and enthusiasm so that Nathan George can face life's challenges with resilience and optimism? *I do*   (0.20)

PAUSE <<< Mom & Dad please repeat together after me: *We promise to cherish and nurture Nathan George throughout his life.*

We promise to guide Nathan George- to respect and support the choices he makes.

We promise to do our best to raise Nathan George - to take his place in the community as a kind and caring person.   (1.0)

9

INSTRUCTIONS   **OFFICIANT**   READINGS   TIMINGS

The Family Celebrant & Officiant

" BESPOKE YOUR CEREMONY "

The ribbon is then systematically wrapped from Edna's left wrist to the two life mentors:
Uncle Jon Henderson and then Aunt Samantha Cohen.

PAUSE <<< Jon and Samantha you both have been chosen and have accepted the responsibility of mentorship for Nathan George Henderson. Given this fact so to confirm; I want to formally ask you both: (0.28)

PAUSE <<< Will you stay close to Nathan George to the best of your ability? *We will* (0.10)

PAUSE <<< Will you help to guide him through life so that he may know the best way you know?
We will (0.15)

PAUSE <<< Will you try to be a good influence by your own way of living, encourage him to observe worthy principles, and decent treatment of his fellow human beings and his world? *We will*
(0.20)

The ribbon is then wrapped from Samantha's left wrist to Philip & Phillipa Cohen; systematically then to Margaret & Greg Henderson, as well as anyone else wishing too; that might have been assembled for this event.

Promises for the remaining and grand parents everyone

PAUSE <<< Mom and dad are very aware that raising a child holds big responsibilities. It is important that they are able to ask for support on occasions, and for Nathan George to be able to gain counsel from family and friends

- people he can trust to go to as he grows.
- As they say, it takes a village to raise a child. (0.30)

INSTRUCTIONS   OFFICIANT   READINGS   TIMINGS

Ceremony Guide   CSOC

"BESPOKE YOUR CEREMONY"

PAUSE <<< With this in mind, mom and dad have chosen to invite all of you here today – to make an affirmation that you will help guide and nurture Nathan George from helpless babyhood into independent adulthood.

Will you help to offer Nathan George *a broad and balanced view of life,* We will   (0.26)

PAUSE <<< *Will you encourage him in the virtues we all agree as good - integrity, honesty, concern, fairness and love toward his fellow human beings.* We will   (0.20)

PAUSE <<< Will you be a shoulder for mom and dad to lean on when they need it? We will   (0.15)

PAUSE <<< *Will you accept Nathan George into your community and welcome him into your hearts?* We will.   (0.15)

When everyone has been "wrapped" the loose end is then fastened into another loop and placed around the right wrist of the child to be named – thus completing the circle. The child is then given their "forever name".

PAUSE <<<< Nathan George – happy little spirit. Smiling child, we wish you joy; health; strength; love and peace On this your special naming day.   (0.15)

PAUSE <<<< Nathan George – lively little boy.

Perfect child, we send you our blessings for a long and happy life, energy and freedom, On this your special naming day.   (0.20)

PAUSE <<<< Nathan George – our love goes out to you precious child with eyes so wide, waving arms and dancing feet, and busy hands which hold so tight on this your special naming day   (0.20)

INSTRUCTIONS   OFFICIANT   READINGS   TIMINGS

The Family Celebrant & Officiant

" BESPOKE YOUR CEREMONY "

PAUSE <<<< We would like everyone to join in with a poem of wishes for his future: *We wish for you the following:*
For beauty to enlighten you and happiness to uplift you,
Wonder amaze you and love fulfil you.
For your step to be certain and your arms be empowered,
For your heart to be open and your words to be peaceful.
For your awareness to grow ambitious in the experience for more.
We wish for you to live in freedom, and may you love - always.

(1.00)

Conclusion

PAUSE <<<< As we draw this ceremony to a close I say to you, Nathan George, may life's richest joys and blessings be yours. May you grow in health of body and mind to full adulthood and may it be your good fortune to play some worthy part in making life more pleasant for those whose paths you cross.

(0.38)

PAUSE <<<< On behalf of dad & mom I'd like to thank you for your attendance, affirmations and support in the past, present and future. We'll end with 1 final poem by mom called "My Son"

(0.24)

Ceremony Guide					CSOC

" BESPOKE YOUR CEREMONY "

Edna:

<u>My Son</u>

Walk gracefully with praise
And appreciate by being grateful.
Do not be deceived by criticism to condemn your path.
My son be approving and not hostile
Learn to relate with compassion and not with fight.
Ridicule, shame and guilt are non negotiable standards.
Meet tolerance with the striving of your desires
and learn to be patient.
My Son, dream big
Be encouraged by faith
and learn to climb with confidence.
My Son, be fair
and you will learn justice.
Security in your highest knowing,
to like yourself.
Acceptance and friendship,
will find you love in the world.

(1.10)

Beautiful boy John Lennon 4:01

Total time of ceremony roughly 30 minutes

13

INSTRUCTIONS   **OFFICIANT**   READINGS   **TIMINGS**

The Family Celebrant & Officiant

Anatomy of A Ceremony   START

Contact: Edna 467 976 4821 ecohenderson@hotmail.com   Ceremony Type: FUN/WED/ROV/NAM

Client(s): The Hendersons   Venue: 6095 Dickenson Rd. E Hamilton Date: 27 / 03 / 2018

Officiant's Responsibilities On The Day	Responsibility of Others
arrive at the Henderson's residence 15 minutes before.	Baby Baby Amy Grant 3:55
look at the set up to make certain music and props ready to go.	Music is turned on and playing
Meet & Greet	
- Admin (asking to switch off all gadgets etc..)	Family has gathered and looks ready
- 1:30pm start to read the "Welcome" poem	
- Intro of officiant & speech	
Scene In ~ Explain a brief history of this type of ceremony.	- Shovels (4) and ready with gum tree everyone near off to the side where it will be planted.
- start giving child & parent history that brought us to this gathering.	
give an explanation/ORDER OF THE TREE PLANTING CEREMONY	1st Element: Tree Planting Ceremony
The Story ~ give a brief history about the ceremony's origins.	Edna; Reggie; Jon and Samantha grab shovels where the mark spot is
give a brief history of the child's name and meaning and how it all ties into with the tree planting.	Reader 1 Reads ~Greg starts with the adapt Jewish Version of a prayer
	Edna makes the first dig and then Reggie.

© 2018 Canadian Society of Celebrants

Ceremony Guide — CSOC

Anatomy of A Ceremony

I thank Greg and Margaret as I invite Philip and Phillipa to come read the remaining last verse.	Reader 2 Reads ~Margaret continues from where Greg left off in the prayer reading out loud.
To finalize off the planting with a blessing; I read an excerpt from the Babylonian *Talmud* Ta'anit 23a "The Story of the Planter"	1st split verse into paragraph to read is Reader 3 Reads ~Philip and last paragraph Reader 4 Reads ~ Phillipa.
Element 1	Jon and Samantha get little Nathan George to help cover the tree with dirt, grab tree, hold it & touch into the earth(ritualistically) **The tree is planted.**
2nd **Element:** The Story ~ give a brief history explain the remodelling to include and combine the naming and promise vows for the child.	**The Ribbon Ceremony**
grab and make ready the blue/silk ribbon and start unrolling at one end to fasten a loop & fit over the left wrist of the child to be named.	Nathan George is called forth by these names & is to go to the Officiant to have his left wrist fastened.
- Officiant starts with the 1st of 4 verses from the naming ceremony unto child.	The ribbon is wrapped around the boy's father Reggie's left wrist.
Reggie is asked to make a promise and then I tie him to the child.	Ribbon is then wrapped around the boy's mother Edna's left wrist.
I ask Edna to make a promise and then wrap her to Reggie.	Edna and Reggie will look directly at the boy and repeat after celebrant.
When all 3 are fastened by the left wrist I ask both Reggie and Edna to look at their little boy and repeat after me some promissory words to him.	**ribbon is then systematically wrapped from Edna's left wrist to Uncle Jon and Aunt Samantha**
- I invite both Jon and Samantha	
- I ask them some promissory words	

© 2018 Canadian Society of Celebrants   2

The Family Celebrant & Officiant

Anatomy of A Ceremony

- Promises for the remaining and grand parents/everyone I give a little brief of what Edna & Reggie would expect from them for the child and then ask them to comply with answer yes/no.	The ribbon is then wrapped from Samantha's left wrist to Philip & Phillipa; systematically then to Margaret & Greg as well as anyone else wishing to; that might have been assembled for this event.
I finish off from where I had started to read the last 3 verses of the naming acknowledgement in blessing confirmation.	Loose end is then fastened into another loop and placed around the right wrist of the child to be named - thus completing the circle.
I ask everyone to join me in a poem to wish Nathan George Henderson many blessings for the future.	Everyone unfastens from Ribbon
-Closing Speech	Reader 5 Reads ~ **Edna reads poem**
I then invite Edna to give a last read from poem called "My Son" by Maria Arvanitidis	
Scene Out Giving Thanks Cue Background Music	Beautiful boy John Lennon 4:01
Signing a commemorative certificate	

FINISH

Ceremony Guide   **CSOC**

Certificate of Naming Day

This is to certify that on this Tuesday, Dated March 27th 2018

1. _____,
Rev/Celebrant, Officiated at the Naming Day of

Nathan George Henderson

Born on Friday the 18th of March 2016
At Harrison Hospital
To Parents *Edna* and *Reggie*

Signature Parent _____ Signature Parent _____
Signature Witness _____ Signature Witness _____
Signature of Rev/Celebrant _____ Dated _____

The Family Celebrant & Officiant

INVOICE #001

DATE: *March 07, 2018*

BILL TO

NAME / *Reggie* Henderson
ADDRESS: 6095 Dickenson Rd. E
............Hamilton 1S7 R6A

PHONE: Edna 467 976 4821

FOR

THE NAMING CEREMONY Package !

Details		AMOUNT
(up to 30 minute) Naming Ceremony package plan		$269.25
4 shovels(4x$4+tax+25%)		$22.60
MayArts/blue/silk/ribbon/Roll (1.5inch/wide&27m/Long)		$28.25
1-CD of ceremonial music ~$10 Signing of commemorative certificate ~ $10	1-	$20.00
	SUBTOTAL	$340.10
	TAX RATE	0.00%
	OTHER	$0.00
	TOTAL	$340.10

THANK YOU FOR YOUR BUSINESS!

Ceremony Guide   CSOC

Peerless Moments
" *BESPOKE YOUR CEREMONY* "

Handfastings, Commitment Ceremonies; Renewals and Baby Naming

CEREMONY PACKAGES: *All Prices Are At Flat Rates*

For newborns/babies/children of all ages, and even pets.
THE NAMING CEREMONY !

From ---$ 359

- Initial Consultation
- Unlimited online interaction and consultations
- A short rehearsal
- Ceremony Design & Script

    Introductions and welcomes -→ Reading or poem
    Reasons for the choice of name→ The naming itself Information about the child(its arrival, personality, interests so far)
    Words about the importance and responsibility of parenting
    Parental promises to the child→ Reading or poem
    Importance of wider family (e.g. grandparents, cousins, etc.)
    The Godparents/relatives; "guide parents,"
    "supporting adults," "mentors" or "special friends".

- Closing statement
- Might want a final read/poem by friends
- Signing a commemorative certificate(can include mentors and/or separately for each).

    . THE ABOVE ELEMENTS/PRODUCTS AS SUBJECT TO COST EXTRA & ARE ONLY GIVEN AS EXAMPLES!
    * TRAVEL EXPENSES ~ $2/KM IF OVER 30 KM TO VENUE/CLIENT.

    NOTE: 25% NON-REFUNDABLE DEPOSIT PAYABLE BY IN PERSON OR ON LINE BEFORE STARTING. FINAL AGREED INVOICE TO BE PAID IN FULL ON COMPLETION AND BEFORE THE CEREMONY IS TO TAKE PLACE.

The Family Celebrant & Officiant

Naming Ceremony/Interview Checklist & Questionnaire

The following Questionnaire will further help to Create for a Unique Naming Day Ceremony:

The following information you provide will help to better clarify with the Interview Checklist(also provided with package)and that might have been missed; overlooked and/or or not clearly made to uncover.
All questions in their entirety will help very much; however

feel free to leave questions you do not feel comfortable answering, and/or things that you do not want mentioned in your ceremony.
Any questions, please let us know!

Name of person completing this form:

Email

The first set of questions might not be included with the interview checklist and can help with the format of your ceremony

Full Name of Parent/s:

Full Name/s and age/s of any other children:

Number of Guests:

PA system (microphone/music) required? (Usually use PA for 30+ guests)

Yes, please

No, thank you

© 2018 Canadian Society of Celebrants

Ceremony Guide   CSOC

Naming Ceremony/Interview Checklist & Questionnaire

The following Questionnaire will further help to Create for a Unique Naming Day Ceremony:

Do you have Godparents / Supporting Adults / Mentors / Life Guides for your child?

Yes

No

If yes, what are their name/s?

Please circle the appropriate above title and/or add to it as preferred.

What will be their title?

Would you like any music to be played before / during / after the ceremony?

Yes, please

No, thank you

If yes, please provide song choice(s) and when you would like it played:

On the Interview Checklist attached with this Questionnaire:

Would you like an Acknowledgement of Land or any other cultural ritual?

Yes, please

No, thank you

If yes, please provide details:

The Family Celebrant & Officiant

Naming Ceremony/Interview Checklist & Questionnaire

The following Questionnaire will further help to Create for a Unique Naming Day Ceremony:

Would you like to acknowledge any absent or deceased family members or friends?

Yes, please

No, thank you

If yes, please provide their name/s and relationship to your child:

Would you like a ritual performed during the ceremony (eg. lighting a candle, releasing helium balloons or butterflies, guest wishing cards, planting a tree, sealing a time capsule, presenting a gift etc.)? *If yes, please provide in detail these choice(s) and when:*
On the Interview Checklist attached with this Questionnaire:

Yes, please

No, thank you

NOTE* : ~ It is recommended for family to be made responsible in providing the supplies for use on the day of and/or make prior arrangements on the extra negotiating prices incurred.

What is your reason for having a Naming Ceremony?

Do you have a family mantra / motto / value statement you would like mentioned?

Yes

No

If yes, please provide details:

© 2018 Canadian Society of Celebrants

Ceremony Guide   CSOC

Naming Ceremony/Interview Checklist & Questionnaire

The following Questionnaire will further help to Create for a Unique Naming Day Ceremony:

Do you have any family heritage or traditions you would like mentioned?

Yes, please

No, thank you

If yes, please provide details:

Would you like any excerpts/readings / poems / songs you would like included?

Yes, please

No, thank you

If so, what would you like include and who would you like to deliver it/them?, *please provide in detail these choice(s) and when: On the Interview Checklist attached with this Questionnaire:*

Would you like a Declaration of your child's name and its history?

Yes, please

No, thank you

If you know the history, provide details here or *On the Interview Checklist attached with this Questionnaire:*(please feel free to ask for our time to help and/or to further do the research).

The Family Celebrant & Officiant

Naming Ceremony/Interview Checklist & Questionnaire

The following Questionnaire will further help to Create for a Unique Naming Day Ceremony:

Would you like to include Vows/Promises by parents / siblings / grand parents / supporting adults?

Yes, please

No, thank you

If so, what format would you like them to be delivered? *please provide in detail these choice(s):   On the Interview Checklist attached with this Questionnaire:*

Question and answer - "Do you promise..." "I do/will" Statements "I promise to love..."

Please provide Vow/Promise wording for Parents:

Please provide Vow/Promise wording for Siblings:

Please provide Vow/Promise wording for Grandparents:

Please provide Vow/Promise wording for Supporting Adults (Godparents):

Would you like to thank or acknowledge siblings, grandparents or any other family members? *please provide in detail these choice(s): On the Interview Checklist attached with this Questionnaire:*

Yes, please

No, thank you

© 2018 Canadian Society of Celebrants

Ceremony Guide   CSOC

Naming Ceremony/Interview Checklist & Questionnaire

The following Questionnaire will further help to Create for a Unique Naming Day Ceremony:

Would you like a toast during the ceremony? *please provide in detail these choice(s): On the Interview Checklist attached with this Questionnaire:*

Yes, please

No, thank you

How many certificates would you like, and

Who will they be for?

Child

Siblings

Grandparents

Supporting Adults/Godparents

Would you like a brief history/story about your child (their personal story, any funny moments or milestones)?

Yes, please

No, thank you

If so, *please answer the following questions*:

This second set of questions helps us to write for 'Your Little Ones Story' & section of the ceremony.

The Family Celebrant & Officiant

Naming Ceremony/Interview Checklist & Questionnaire

The following Questionnaire will further help to Create for a Unique Naming Day Ceremony:
This second set of questions helps us to write for 'Your Little Ones Story' & section of the ceremony.

please answer the following questions:

For a brief story about your child (personal story, any funny moments or milestones).

How did your child arrive into the world?

What were your first thoughts when you meet your child for the first time?

How and why did you choose your Child's name?

What kind of baby/child have they been so far?

What are your hopes and dreams for your child's future?

Ceremony Guide — CSOC

Naming Ceremony/Interview Checklist & Questionnaire

The following Questionnaire will further help to Create for a Unique Naming Day Ceremony:
This second set of questions helps us to write for 'Your Little Ones Story' & section of the ceremony.

please answer the following questions:

List a couple of wonderful, cute, amazing, fun things or stories you have of your child?

What kind of activities and things does your child love to do? (Suck toes, Big wet kisses, Roll over, Chase the dog. ect)

Tell us about your child's sibling/s and their relationship.

If you only had three words to describe your child, what would they be?

What does being a parent mean to you?

The Family Celebrant & Officiant

Naming Ceremony/Interview Checklist & Questionnaire

The following Questionnaire will further help to Create for a Unique Naming Day Ceremony:

Don't be afraid to include any other information we haven't covered that may be important to you and your child's story!

This third set of questions can help us to write about the Supporting Adult / Godparent/s you have chosen:

Supporting Adult / Godparent One:

Supporting Adult / Godparent Two:

Supporting Adult / Godparent Three:

Supporting Adult / Godparent Four:

Is there anything else you would like to be included in the ceremony that hasn't been covered?

© 2018 Canadian Society of Celebrants

Ceremony Guide — CSOC

Naming Ceremony/Interview Checklist & Questionnaire

MAIN CLIENT CONTACT:	
Name	Age
Address	
Email	
Phone	
CEREMONY FOR:	
1)	
2)	
3)	
Date & Time	/ / :
Venue	
Baby Naming / Child Naming / Naming	
BIRTH DETAILS: 1)	
Date	Age
Place	

The Family Celebrant & Officiant

Naming Ceremony/Interview Checklist & Questionnaire

BIRTH DETAILS: 2)	
Date	Age
Place	

BIRTH DETAILS: 3)	
Date	Age
Place	

SPOUSE / PARTNER	
Name	Age
Where Met	Date
Where Married	Date
History	

Ceremony Guide   **CSOC**

Naming Ceremony/Interview Checklist & Questionnaire

FRIENDS & RELATIVES
Parents
Brothers
Sisters
Grandparents
Close Friends / Life Mentor
Other Children
OTHER RELEVANT DETAILS / CEREMONY REQUIREMENTS **Parent / Guardian Promises**   **Life Mentor Promises**   **Other Promises**

The Family Celebrant & Officiant

Naming Ceremony/Interview Checklist & Questionnaire

CEREMONY PARTICULARS
Music
Images: Photos / CD / DVD / AV / Power Point
SPECIAL ELEMENTS
Readings / Poetry

Ceremony Guide   CSOC

Naming Ceremony/Interview Checklist & Questionnaire

OTHER SPEAKERS
REFRESHMENTS
Where & When?
Notes

The Family Celebrant & Officiant
Chapter Three ~ Child Naming/Blessing Ceremony

Naming's/Blessings: They do not have to be religious, even a baptism can become a ceremony onto its own. It might make more sense however; to accept the minister, that is paid by the church and when renting for such venues. Unlike the religious official, who is commissioned by the church; the celebrant is not included in the church's price. A secular ceremony, is unique; in that it is created especially for a particular family and their circumstances. This means there is no set script and no fixed structure. Instead, the celebrant will be the guide; as the celebrant you must learn how to lead the family, through the various options. Help them to trust you enough, to open up and create an occasion that's fitting for their specific circumstances. Whatever your structure is, the package for a naming ceremony; the following are pointers to better simplify the order:

Introductions and welcomes -→ Reading or poem
Reasons for the choice of name→ The naming itself Information about the child(its arrival, personality, interests so far)
Words about the importance and responsibility of parenting
Parental promises to the child→ Reading or poem
Importance of wider family (e.g. grandparents, cousins, etc.)
The Godparents/relatives; "guide parents,"
"supporting adults," "mentors" or "special friends".
Have them join in the ceremony, to express how they will be there for the child; how they will play an influential role in its life. Promises to the child are also made by the family, supporting adults and can include all other attendees.
They can be repeated as statements led by the celebrant; or the celebrant can pose ceremonial questions to the guests(various forms are possible).

Concluding words !
Other ideas too, are always welcomed......

Chapter Three ~ Child Naming/Blessing Ceremony

The following is yet another, more traditional to sample from:

An outline of the ceremony

Intro Opening (Welcome)
explanation of the celebration
Opening Prayer of Blessing
Inspirational or Scripture Reading
Motivational Moment
Charge to Parents
Affirmation of Parents
Charge to godparents
Affirmation of godparents
Charge to Friends and Family
Affirmation of Friends and Family
Anointing of Child
Prayer of Dedication
Presentation of Certificate

Closing Words

Canadian Society Of Celebrants, is designed, to guide the celebrant and with supportive training, along their experience. Not every family will be aligned perfectly with you nor any other particular religion or faith group. For this reason the more informed we are as celebrants, the more we can enlighten for those who don't know what they want; but wish to have a special day and a memorable ceremony. A naming ceremony does not have to be held in a church nor is it just for babies.

People of all ages and namely children over the age of 13 months, all the way up to puberty and beyond.

A naming ceremony, can have many suitable venues and are not just limited to churches and peoples homes.

A park and/or natural setting can make for a great home welcoming and name blessing initiation.

The Family Celebrant & Officiant

Chapter Three ~ Child Naming/Blessing Ceremony

It is the perfect moment to become the supportive space and trust that the youth will find comfort and security in knowing to believe in this group. This special day that is set aside to celebrate the kind of commitment that it involves to confirm with others and make the oath; in their involvement and that they will share in contribution, of investing promises in this youth.

A baptism style ceremony and that can include anointing of your favourite fragrance alchemy oil can be included.

It can be performed in a body of water, where the child can be immersed; rather dipped in. This can be in the same body of water; or nearby, where the mother had given birth to the child. When anointing the child it can be on the wrists and feet and in between the eyes above the forehead; the navel and the heart and throat and anywhere else that might add to the scripted explanation of this ceremonial element.

The fragrance can be of a combination or anything you wish to add for its meaning can also be included in the script.

A sigil or an inscription to anoint with; rather than a cross or plane dot or circle. So many options to choose and decide this special day with. Although these books and teachings prefer the student to learn how to modify and adapt to its own.

Sometimes a script can carry with it, an inauthentic substance; it is alright to add these credits in. When the family wishes to make extra copies and for public use; the creative rights must be purchased or removed. The rules that have been made, are anything over the 80 year mark; that has not been given over to another party and in the selling over of its rights, is and can be copy rights approved, for all intents and purposes.

Ceremony Guide   CSOC

Chapter Three ~ Child Naming/Blessing Ceremony

Ultimately we must strive to please; in the reaffirming of what the family unit, believe and value. To illustrate their values they wish to instill; as well as any ties that need to be highlighted between the parents, child and godfather/mother and other wishes from all the attendees. The ceremony can include many ritual acts (symbolic movements) to select from and be integrated. Fingerprinting leaves on a tree drawing to add on a piece of canvas and then signed by all participants. It is also possible to include a gift exchange moment to the event; as well as the signature of a symbolic godfather/mother certificate.
From involved rituals and symbolism, to readings and poems; speeches in the form of texts and poems may be read, with background music and/or by singing.
The following are some samples to add to your selection.

Religious & secular readings for child naming ceremonies

The Little Children and Jesus
(The Roles of Faith & Trust)
Bible (Mark 10:13-16) KJV

[13] And they brought young children to him, that he should touch them: and his disciples rebuked those that brought them.

[14] But when Jesus saw it, he was much displeased, and said unto them, Suffer the little children to come unto me, and forbid them not: for of such is the kingdom of God.

[15] Verily I say unto you, whosoever shall not receive the kingdom of God as a little child, he shall not enter therein.

[16] And he took them up in his arms, put his hands upon them, and blessed them.

The Family Celebrant & Officiant
Chapter Three ~ Child Naming/Blessing Ceremony
Religious & secular readings for child naming ceremonies

Your children are not your children

By_Kahlil Gibran (1883-1931)

Your children are not your children.
They are the sons and daughters of life's longing for itself.
They come through you but not from you,
And though they are with you yet they belong not to you.
You may give them your love but not your thoughts,
For they have their own thoughts.
You may house their bodies but not their souls,
For their souls dwell in the house of tomorrow, which you cannot visit, not even in your dreams.
You may strive to be like them, but seek not to make them like you.
For life goes not backward nor tarries with yesterday.
You are the bows from which your children as living arrows are sent forth.
The archer sees the mark upon the path of the infinite,
and bends you with might that the arrows may go swift and far.
Let your bending in the Archer's hand be for gladness;
For even as the Archer loves the arrow that flies,
so the Archer also loves the bow that is stable.

Chapter Three ~ Child Naming/Blessing Ceremony

Religious & secular readings for child naming ceremonies

A Prayer Celebrating the spirit of a child

(Anonymous)

Give us the consciousness of a child.
Give us the child who lives within
– the child who trusts, the child who dreams,
the child who sings, the child who doesn't hold back
from divine free will, the child who receives without judgment.
Give us a child's perception, to project the beauty
and freshness of this day like a sunrise.
Give us a child's thoughts, that we may hear
the music of mythical times.
Give us a child's memory, that we may be filled
with wonder and delight.
Give us a child's imagination,
that we may be cured of our cynicism.
Give us the light of the child,
too innocent to be afraid
and naive enough to show the need for love.

Amen

The Family Celebrant & Officiant
Chapter Three ~ Child Naming/Blessing Ceremony

Religious & secular readings for child naming ceremonies

All Things Bright and Beautiful

Cecil Frances Alexander (1818-1895)

(Refrain)Chorus:
All things bright and beautiful,
All creatures great and small,
All things wise and wonderful,
The Lord God made them all.

1. Each little flower that opens,
   Each little bird that sings,
   He made their glowing colours,
   and made their tiny wings.
   (*Refrain*/*Chorus*)

2. The purple-headed mountains,
   the river running by,
   the sunset and the morning
   that brightens up the sky.
   (Refrain)

3. The cold wind in the winter,
   the pleasant summer sun,
   the ripe fruits in the garden,
   God made them every one.
   (Refrain)

4. He gave us eyes to see them,
   and lips that we might tell
   how great is God Almighty,
   who has made all things well.
   (Refrain)

Chapter Three ~ Child Naming/Blessing Ceremony

Religious & secular readings for child naming ceremonies

The following was modified and taken from a Native American Blessing(to teach the reader how to adapt and further make use of).

Nature homecoming

All planets, big and small and that move within this field,
can hear the name, that we are to give to this child!
Into your midst anew we give this child.
Welcome it home and as your own, to learn in trust
and be lifted up all the hills in its life!
Winds, Clouds, Rain, Mist, all you that move in the air, hear us!
Welcome into your midst this name.
refresh and sooth/this child as your own, by this name to trust
and in the flow up all the hills in its life be carried!
All you of the earth, hear this name!
Into your midst this new name for our child.
Embrace and as your own to welcome home / to learn in trust
and be lifted up all the hills!
Birds, great and small, that fly in the air,
Fish that swim in all your depths large and small.
All creatures, great and small, that dwell in the forest;
that creep among the grasses and burrow in the ground, to hear this name!
Into your midst this new name we give to our child.
Welcome home this child as your own, to learn in trust and be lifted up all the hills!
May the heavens open to welcome, the air, and earth, to hear this name now!
Into your midst this new name we give to our child.
Welcome home this child as your own, to learn in trust and be lifted up all the hills! ~ Author unknown

The Family Celebrant & Officiant
The Lamb   From (Hindu Vedas)
<u>The Upanishads</u>

Lead us from death to life,
From falsehood to truth;
Lead us from despair to hope,
From fear to trust;
Lead us from hate to love,
From war to peace;
Let peace fill our hearts,
Our world, our universe.

<u>Efficient & Effective</u>

The more information you can get on your celebrity for the day; the more relevant and meaningful the script.
Unless you personally know the family and the child; you will need to creatively come up with as many questions, to fill in your draft with. Otherwise the unavoidable revising over it again, will take place and just as much time, if not more to clarify.
The more you can find out and get a better feel of the family's wishes and concerns; the more you can advise and make for better suggestions. Also the financial amount of interest, to invest and that the family, is willing to spend; it will determine just how involved, they wish and for you to be. Rather than giving them too much information, find out how easy it is and how much information, you can get out of them; otherwise they will, more than likely, be shopping around and go somewhere else.
Just remember, playing can be fun and as long as people wish to play with us; otherwise we get played. When engaging with your clients, try to assess their character. Just think of the interaction and get a feel of the amount of involvement, that they will wish to spare; like taking a really long shower and/or many little ones, in the engagement with them.

Chapter Four:

Nuptials And The Undoing & Parting of Ways Ceremony

What are the Celebrant's Responsibilities Here In Canada?

Clergy Vs. Celebrant

The only case scenario and where it makes a difference; is in the legalization of marriage and sometimes within the parting of ways. In this study, religious officials we are not and the legal pronouncements and documentation provided for witnessing the matrimony are not of our concern. In most cases, it has become good business and to provide the bare minimum; but it is not a Celebrant, that these couples are interested in.

Perhaps these couples might realize eventually; their regrets, in not affording themselves a silly ceremony, and fork out the money to renew their vows. This will be discussed in the next chapter to come. The Celebrant always has the advantage; however not so much value is given to them. Perhaps it is because of the lack of awareness; that the client might be given and to evaluate the interest for the opportunities. Rather in this way the playing field is balanced.

Canadian Society Of Celebrants, is not subject only to Judeo-Christian and most importantly, not limited to Abrahamic structures of belief systems. In many cases it is a civil ceremony that we provide; because performing the ceremony, does not require that it be registered and by any official licensing body.

The Family Celebrant & Officiant
What are the Celebrant's Responsibilities Here In Canada ?

Clergy Vs. Celebrant

Although Agnostic was not mentioned here, to take into consideration and from the many other non Abrahamic philosophies: Canadian Society Of Celebrants honours all individual beliefs and idealisms of spiritual expression; including Agnostic/Humanist and Atheist (to be recognized and valued for their painful and emotional needs as well). In order to have the ability we must learn their ways of preference and from here everything can better be more simplified. Agnostics tend to lean toward the unknown and make it known. Agnostic has got to be one of the oldest religions into faith and the unknowable truths. It can bring much depth to any ceremony and script; by bringing certainty into the unknown mysteries and able to grasp them into meaningful experiences. Atheists are quite similar to Humanists in their services; however the religious author's aspects are replaced with legal significances.

Semi-Secular Vs. Secular:

We must distinguish here our roles and that we play for any given event(look up volume one, for more). A religious official, is only really ever required and in the case of a legal matrimony; not for a wedding/commitment ceremony celebration. In the same way, a lawyer is required for the legal un-doings; however in the case of separation/divorce and where, a Celebrant can provide, a marriage undoing ceremony service. A wedding planner, is similar to a caterer and this is not our job description either; however we can only be informed and as well as the Anatomy of A Ceremony can better to reflect(the event planner is who we must be fully engaging with to find out).

Chapter Four:
Nuptials And The Undoing & Parting of Ways Ceremony

What are the Celebrant's Responsibilities Here In Canada ?

Semi-Secular Vs. Secular:

Always make certain that you are connected and in the loop with your client's wishes, for your services. Other than these few things; a semi-secular collaboration with a religious official, must be kept separated. As Celebrants, we can only declare the marriage and pronounce it in a certain way; do not put yourselves in such a dilemma, unless you are the religious official.
More will be discussed to clear up the confusion.
We are not subject or bound to secular matters; rather as Canadian Celebrants and residing in Canada, we can perform collaboratively and semi-secularly.

The Sum of History:
In some commonwealth places; such as Australia, Celebrants are obligated and remain under the Marriage Act of 1961.
The Notice of Intended Marriage form(NOIM), is commonly filled out and accompanied by form 14, for a Statutory Declaration(having no legal impediment signed statement); that must be filed(good for up to 18 months, to get married) with the Celebrant. Although it is possible to speculate(how its origins as a Celebrant did come about); to suggest, for a greater probability and of having to become a licensed body, here in Canada someday, as in Australia. As greatly respected non-secular bodies are and with their religious rites; Australian Celebrants too, are equally licensed, as secular entities and given the legal authority, to perform marriages. From there, the history of Celebrants, has something to be desired; because it started spreading over to the United Kingdom; United States of America and finally started to catch on, here in Canada.

The Family Celebrant & Officiant
What are the Celebrant's Responsibilities Here In Canada ?

Secular and Non-Secular :

In Australia, they are exactly authorized and as a religious official, here in Canada would be. Similar to a marriage licence; a marriage cannot be solemnized. Unless a notice in writing of the intended marriage, and in the prescribed form, is given to the authorized Celebrant and who is solemnizing the marriage. The authorized Celebrant and to whom the notice is given, sends the notice to the Registrar of Births, Deaths and Marriages, of the State or Territory; in which the marriage takes place and well after the marriage ceremony. In Canada, there is no such acknowledgement, as of yet; however a religious official, must keep a record for the Crown of this intent(blue book). The licence, is already in the same, however broken into these two parts(licence and blue book). This documented intent, is given to the department; that then services the government to issue the approval of the licence. The religious official or a justice of the peace must then fill out the appropriated places and sign the marriage licence. In this case the Celebrant is not really of any value as of yet; however most of the templates for these kind of ceremonies, have been taken and modified from their point of origin/source. Spirituality does not have to become hijacked and bound by these principles; nor by previous recordings and to form its structure by them for a celebration.

As Canadian celebrants, we are not subject to any of the monastic confinements; nor does the word "Secularism" to suggest that we must be an Ethical Union of Humanist Societies. By omitting this kind of postulants in our Celebrants, we can serve all walks of life; including the Atheist(non-secular/secular confused) Political "Mad Hatters" and Agnostics.

Chapter Four:

What are the Celebrant's Responsibilities Here In Canada ?

Secular and Non-Secular :

Canadian Society Of Celebrants, can incorporate much more meaningful "religious" methods and non-secular beliefs; with the interfaith and all other such non-denominational ministry affiliations alike. Always know your place within the thick of it, your mission and the duties and obligations that have been asked from you by the couple. The mission of your engagement and the role you play in all of this; it must be well defined and given healthy boundaries to achieve. We are simple servants, with less creative limitations and to aspire others with unconditional self expression. Freedom is the key to "Soul" and the ability to express it, in a more subtle and spiritual way. This is, at the source of its enlightenment and motive to inspire; the pristine aspects, from all religious conglomerations. "Faith" does not require a religion; however religion does require a certain level of "Faith".
At the apex of such a unconventional approach and that a Secular Celebrant or even non can find resonance to.
The Celebrant, by no means are they a HAT(non-secular community) "Humanist" and have no obligations as of yet by legal bind to licence. A celebrant can offer their services anywhere (even off planet) with no conditional limits and can be civil, as well as faith transparent. This is where, we stand out and differ from the rest of the pack. In this way by learning and eliminating from what we are not, we can begin to make more sense of what we are and what we can and cannot offer. What makes Canadian Society Of Celebrants different and in this even most subtle of ways, we can get to know our titles better.

The Family Celebrant & Officiant
Nuptials And The Undoing & Parting of Ways Ceremony

"THE ROLE OF CEREMONY"
(defining who we are; by knowing what we are not).

"Throughout history, in countries all over the world, ceremonies have been used to mark important events, in people's lives. Many, though and by no means all; we find that a formal occasion of this kind, can be very helpful. (As this was discussed in the previous book of volume one)An Atheist service, can be held at any time(please refer to volume-one, for further knowledge).
At a Humanist wedding the couple have the opportunity to declare publicly their love for each other and their aspirations for their future together. They can make this commitment among their family and friends in a meaningful and significant ceremony. The Humanist concept of a wedding ceremony is quite distinctive. It illuminates important values and beliefs; while giving expression to the two people's personalities. Moreover, there is a flexibility and openness of approach that is quite unusual. Remarriage after divorce, the marriage of couples where children from earlier relationships are included, weddings where the bride does not wish to be 'given away' by her father or to take her husband's name — all kinds of different situations can be accommodated. Quite often the couple choose a very traditional ceremony, merely omitting the religious elements they would feel to be hypocritical." Canadian Society Of Celebrants, is rather, more similar to its Civil Celebrants; however it does not limit to omit or redefine religious content and even to take it to the next level of reveal. We welcome all ideas and including religious and cultural beliefs, from all walks of life.
A recent increasingly popular and preferred alternative to a Humanist service is a civil ceremony. This is also a non-religious ceremony and completely neutral in its delivery.

Chapter Four:
Nuptials And The Undoing & Parting of Ways Ceremony

Atheist/Humanist and Civil Celebrants:

Aside from the egalitarian and legal authorization of matrimony(to recite under the Marriage Act), that the Atheist/Humanist can offer; it might be thought, that there is no other real significant difference, between them and our Canadian Society Of Celebrants. Whilst providing a valid and meaningful non-religious ceremony, the Humanist is under a legal body umbrella of entitlement. It must endorse its Humanist differences and in certain phrases that are used as part of the ceremony. For most people this is not a problem.
It's hardly noticeable(until addressed); because it blends in with the Humanist theme of the ceremony. These type of ceremonies, are not very flexible in their approach and when it comes to religious content, during the ceremony. The saying of a prayer or the reading of a short extract from the bible, then that would not normally be allowed. In the same way that the mixing and blending in of many other faiths and cultural traditional beliefs. What a huge difference Canadian Society of Celebrants can bring to the table of creative offerings. Canadian Society Of Celebrants is the next level of configuration; to accept from the many infinite possibilities of a unified field, where everything can come together creatively for processing. Specifically derived, and from the core essence of what it means to be Canadian.
With the soul expression, of Canada in mind and is something, like no other of its kind.

The Family Celebrant & Officiant

What a Humanist Order of Ceremony might look like:

(prelude music) *THE OPENING STATEMENT

As it continues on and with a humane belief, of doing no harm; by bringing in so many words and the acceptance of this partnership. Consenting adult 1._____ and 2._____ are willingly accepting to be married under a human institution; that finds its deepest meaning in the celebration of being human.

*I Do's for the parents(giving of their blessing)

*The couples pledge

Do you both, as humanly as possible accept, this reality to be truth ?

*Officiant's ADVICE TO THE COUPLE

Your pledge today of your devotion. As spoken, will validate your marriage and only when you, yourselves believe.

*The commitment announcement and solemn declaration

*EXCHANGE OF VOWS

I call upon these persons here present to witness that I, 1._____/2._____ , do take you, 2._____ /1._____, to be my lawful wedded wife/husband.

*THE EXCHANGE OF RINGS

*INTERLUDE

THE SIGNING OF THE MARRIAGE LICENCE AND REGISTER

*A Mindful Moment of Thoughtfulness(blessings)

*THE SECOND READING

*THE PRONOUNCEMENT

*THE KISS

THE INTRODUCTION OF THE COUPLE TO THE GATHERING finally after the couple are married and walk back down the aisle (recessional music).

What do you do when a couple is interested in your services? The following sample can help, to guide you along this process.

Ceremony Guide   CSOC

Chapter Four:

The following guide, is a combination and of just how explicit, a Celebrant's delivery must be; blended in with a Religious (Ontario) Official's package. Make an observation, on how these officiating titles, might be similar and get a feel, from within their differences, as well. Then modify to create your own.

Peerless Moments
"BESPOKE YOUR CEREMONY"

Wedding Packages

Traditional (standard) Ceremony   Fees

Plan, Practice, Perform
- Welcoming Wedding Ceremony package
- Initial Interview (Anatomy of Ceremony) $ 529
  To help clarify the order of the Wedding Proceedings
- Wedding Ceremony Official package
- Draft Order of Ceremony
- Unlimited telephone meetings and online consultations
- 2nd Interview ~ Agree Order of Ceremony & Modify to Final Draft
- Wedding Ceremony script
- Final Interview/rehearsal & visit venue
- Officiate Ceremony (up to 30 min. Average)

Elopement Ceremony.... THE QUICKY ! $ 299

- Brief: Sharing of Vows & Civil Ceremony for the Solemnization Marriage Act Specifics.
- Look after the legal marriage licence
- (optional) A signed proof of marriage keepsake (optional)

Simply Divine Ceremony $ 429

- Welcoming Wedding Ceremony package
- Initial Interview (Anatomy of Ceremony)
  To help clarify the order of the Wedding Proceedings.
- Unlimited telephone meetings and online consultations
- Wedding Ceremony Official package
- option to Officiate Ceremony (up to 20 min. Average with a brief very short rehearsal) And/Or up to 30 min with no rehearsal/A signed proof of marriage keepsake (optional)
- (optional, Copy) Ceremony script
- Look after the legal marriage licence
- NB: 50% Initial Deposit Fee is Payable before starting and with a 25% Non- Refundable.
- Final Agreed Invoice to be paid in full on the day of Ceremony and before the paperwork signing.

The Family Celebrant & Officiant

"BESPOKE YOUR CEREMONY"

Wedding Ceremony Fees

NOTE----- " This is a solemnized performance, under the Ontario marriage ceremony Act ".

under 30 min. CEREMONY on Average

Planning, Practice, Perform – from $529
If over 30 min. (for the more Elaborate) prices can range from $900 to $1000/full hr.

Without Rehearsal~ from $429

THE QUICKY (Elopement Ceremony)------------------------

$299

This is similar to the signing and witnessing: After the couple has received from their local municipality their package; the licence it is valid for up to 90 days for the purpose of this ceremony and to contact the officiant ready to perform. With the original licence the Officiant can fill out and sign (after the service formal ceremony legalities to solemnize the marriage) and then to be signed by the 2 witnesses(maid of honour and best man). All personal data is then entered into the Marriage Register book and must be signed at the ceremony by the couple, the two witnesses and the Officiating Minister. The original licence is then within 48hrs mailed to the Registrars office and keeps a scanned and copied on record for filing and documenting in register book for the crown. The Official Marriage Certificate (In the presentation folder to find or provided how to go online) can be submitted 6 to 8 weeks after the marriage ceremony (this is required as proof for name change and when not Canadian born)..

- **NOTE*-----If any information is deemed inaccurate it will be returned back***

2

Ceremony Guide   CSOC

Chapter Four:

Peerless Moments
"BESPOKE YOUR CEREMONY"

Special Ceremony Elements

Signing & Witness Ceremony -- $ 90
A brief ceremony (after the marriage ceremony) involving the couple and 2-4 witnesses, Each in turn sign a keepsake parchment which is then presented to the newlyweds.

* Note: This is not a legal record marriage certificate *

- NOTE* With some exceptions to pricing:
ALL OTHER UNITY CEREMONY ELEMENTS FROM THE ACTUAL PURCHASE OF PRODUCT WILL HAVE A **35% MARK-UP** FROM THEIR RETAIL PRICE + TAXES INCLUDED; AND FURTHER ENHANCEMENTS TO DESIGN WILL BE FURTHER NEGOTIABLE WITH ALL SAID PARTIES PRIOR TO.

Signing & Witness Ceremony
A brief ceremony involving the couple and 2-4 witnesses, Each in turn sign a keepsake parchment which is then presented to the newlyweds.
* Note: This is not a legal record marriage certificate

Unity Sand Ceremony Option
A great ritual option to involve the children in the joining of the couple.

Wine Box / Love Letter
To write love letters to each other before the wedding then seal in an envelope. At a later time; during an anniversary; or when having thoughts of separating to drink the wine and read the letters so to hopefully remember why the falling in love and choice to be together happened in the first place.

Breaking of the Glass Ceremony
The Breaking of the Glass Ceremony option to signify the end of the ceremony and the time of celebration. As a health & safety concern, the glass (often two champagne flutes) is placed in a cloth bag prior to breaking it.

Smashing Coconuts
From $ 25 for 4 and 25% of the proceeds can go towards the couple as a gift. When the newly weds make there way out so to clear them from any obstacles they might encounter on the new path they will take together.

The Family Celebrant & Officiant
Nuptials And The Undoing & Parting of Ways Ceremony

"BESPOKE YOUR CEREMONY"

Special Ceremony Elements

Wine Ceremony
In the Wine ceremony to either choose to pour one white
glass and one red glass for a blush creation that both can drink from or a
pouring of one glass to both drink from.

Broom Jumping Ceremony
To clear away of negativity with a sweep of the broom and create a threshold to cross over into a new life together. Have the guests write their names on pieces of decorative paper to attach to symbolically binding ribbons, and tie to the broom before it is jumped. These well wishes -- go into the marriage with the couple. The broom can be outfitted beautifully with silk ribbons
Plus fresh or silk flowers, bows, beads and more.......

Rose Petal Ceremony
A ceremony to have a bunch of petals all over the floor so to walk on them and have others toss them at the couples feet.

Dove Release Ceremony
Doves choose one partner for life and make this commitment until death.
 It is said that if doves are seen on your wedding day, a happy home is assured. It is the folklore belief that releasing doves is a ceremony option that signifies new beginnings.

Unity Candle
Used in Catholic weddings, but as a traditional ceremony option it also holds a universal meaning. The joining of in marriage as well as the two original families; so to involve the mothers from each side of the family to light individually these candles for as a symbol to show the moving on from their family to create a new family together.

American Indian Wedding Vase Ceremony
This vase features two openings(drinking spouts) connected by a single handle and symbolizes the union of marriage between two people.
To drink simultaneously without spilling a drop is anticipated to have good understanding with them throughout their marriage.

4

Chapter Four:

"BESPOKE YOUR CEREMONY"

Special Ceremony Elements

CD recorded
Music for the ceremony ------------------------ depending on the music amount and length and quality anything from $15 -$25.

First Kiss Last Kiss
Involves the mother of both sides of the family near the end of the ceremony. The mothers gave their children there first kiss when they came into the world and they will give their last kiss as single individuals before sending them on their new journey as life partners.

Warming of the rings
Passing of the rings. spend a few seconds giving their blessing and well wishes, before passing the rings on to the next person.
With some nice music playing in the background and the time will lapse smoothly.

Group song/s at a wedding and/or a mass reading too
No rehearsals required, no prior knowledge needed.
The wording can also be included on your order of service.
A simple print out of the words on to card or paper (one per pair) can be provided and be placed on the seats prior to the ceremony.

Costs to be Agreed prior to Ceremony

Travel expenses - $2per km if over 30 to venue / client.
Accommodation – At Cost if overnight stay required.
Fancy Dress – At Cost as required
Miscellaneous Costs – As agreed (Reception MC / Toastmaster)

NB: 25% Non-Refundable Deposit Payable at Initial Interview.
Final Agreed Invoice to be paid in Full on completion of Final Interview

The Family Celebrant & Officiant

"BESPOKE YOUR CEREMONY"

Ceremony- Interview Checklist

CONTACT DETAILS
(Exactly as shown on licence, From left to right)
Spouse 1   [ ] Never Married [ ] Widowed [ ] Divorced
Address
Email
Phone
(Exactly as shown on licence, on right side)
Spouse 2   [ ] Never Married [ ] Widowed [ ] Divorced
Address
Email
Phone
CEREMONY FOR:
Full Legal Name _____ Spouse 1
Occupation:
Age [ ] Date Of Birth: Where:
Parent's Name _____
Parent's Name
Full Legal Name _____ Spouse 2
Occupation:
Age [ ] DateOfBirth: Where:
Parent's Name _____
Parent's Name _____

6

Ceremony Guide   CSOC

Nuptials And The Undoing & Parting of Ways Ceremony

Peerless Moments
"BESPOKE YOUR CEREMONY"

Ceremony- Interview Checklist

PARTICIPATING FRIENDS & RELATIVES :		
Witnesses	**Spouse 1** Full Legal Name _____ Address	**Spouse 2** Full Legal Name _____ Address
Grandparents		
Brothers		
Sisters		
Friends		
Children		
Other		

The Family Celebrant & Officiant

"BESPOKE YOUR CEREMONY"

Ceremony- Interview Checklist

Theme?: **Ceremony Officiant dress wear:** Normally with own business brand/Ministry Attire; however (if not acceptable) will cost extra to provide for the certain costume theme? **Agreed Extras:** Costume Hire Travel Accommodation	
Location of Venue?: Time & Day **Please give as many details** (roughly how many are invited) **Accessibility?:** **Contingency?:** **Rehearsal** : **time and day** (who will be there) please make certain to include every participant as well as entertainment…DJ and other(s) as such……	
Specials Elements: Handfasting Unity Ceremony Broom Jumping Rose Ceremony Parchment Ring Warming Other… **Personal vows**	
RING(S) and/or……: **Please explain** (with as much detail) Is there going to be a ring exchange ? and/or just one ring given ?	

Feel free to add additional Q&A lines if needed (if you have something you really want to share that is not listed).

8

Ceremony Guide   CSOC

<u>Nuptials And The Undoing & Parting of Ways Ceremony</u>

Peerless Moments

"BESPOKE YOUR CEREMONY"

<u>About your relationship</u>?

Think about how you felt when you first met, what made you fall in love and when you knew you wanted to spend the rest of your lives together. Write it all out to get your creative gears turning.

A fully customized ceremony will require for the Officiant to design a ceremony that reflects your love story.
A truly a unique ceremony for each couple, and all about you.
It can be religious or non-religious, you decide!
Make your ceremony exactly what you want, and not the stuffy boring ceremony that everyone has seen in the past.

This is a "free type" and the columns will expand as you write.
Do not focus on grammar or structure or even spelling (though feel free to run a spell check before sending back your answers).
Try to be as open as possible and do not worry because anything potentially hurtful and/or embarrassing will not be publicly shared and/or during your ceremony! However, the more information you provide, the more meaningful picture of who you are can become more colourful.

The Family Celebrant & Officiant

"BESPOKE YOUR CEREMONY"

Personalized Vows

Can be written by either or both partners and ==at an extra cost==; you can even ask us, ==to simply write it for you==. Personalized vows can help you express your love for one another and promise to support and love each other for many years to come.

No matter what you choose - be it traditional, religious or personalized vows - remember the focus of your wedding should be on you.

The Wedding Vows / ==What do you prefer==?

Your vows may run from traditional to customized. Feel free to add your own embellishments, loving words, funny promises(I promise to take the trash out!) and inside jokes. Also, couples may like pieces of several of the vow examples, while not finding any one example that completely reflects their preferences. ==Pieces from several can be blended together to make the "perfect" one.== (Please specify by circling 1of 3)

There are 3 formats or "styles" ==for vows (and also **ring exchanges**)==:==Please specify for both==

1. <u>Echo</u> - Officiant says "Please repeat after me", then reads the vow one line at a time, with participant repeating each line, one line at a time, until the vow is complete.

2. <u>I Do</u> - Officiant begins with "Do you", then reads the entire vow, followed by the participant's response of "I do"

3. <u>Recital</u> - a more personal vow, (does not have to be spoken from memory) while looking directly into the partner's eyes, and without prompt by the Officiant.
This format can be tricky, especially if the vows are long and complex.

You don't have to answer every one of the questions below, but it gives you a sense of what you can write about for us. Feel free to add additional Q&A lines (if needed, if you have something you really want to share that is not listed).

PLEASE
do not show your answers of the following below questions to each other – send them only back to us!
We will save a copy of your answers in your file!

10

Ceremony Guide   CSOC

Nuptials And The Undoing & Parting of Ways Ceremony

"BESPOKE YOUR CEREMONY"

Here's a handy list of questions to help get you started:	
Where & How did you meet? What have they been doing since.	
When was your first date and what was it like?	
Do you have any children or pets?	
When did you "know" that they were the right person?	
When did you first say, "I love you?"	
When did you know you wanted to get married? The proposal.	
How did you get engaged?	
What are your nicknames for each other?	
What's something quirky or unique about your relationship?	
What Type of work do you do?	
What do you like to do together? (keep it rated PG)	

The Family Celebrant & Officiant

"BESPOKE YOUR CEREMONY"

What type of music do you like or favourite band?	
What is your favorite food?	
What is your favorite movie and/or TV Show?	
Do you have any "Pet Peeves"?	
Are you "Geeky" about anything?	
Who is your Hero?	
What is your hobby or do you collect things? Pastimes / Hobbies	
What do you do for a living?	
How would you describe your relationship?	
How do you describe your fiancé to people who are hearing about him/her for the first time?	
What, if anything, do you expect to change about your relationship after this wedding (other than more free time, of course)?	
What are you most looking forward to about your life together, after this wedding?	
What do you see when you think about your longer-term future together?	

We know some of the questions are intense. As we mentioned before, you do not have answer all of them. This is meant to be helpful to us and not to make you feel at all uncomfortable.
Your answers will be very helpful in preparing your wedding ceremony.
Remember, do not show your answers to each other – send them only back to us!
We will save a copy of your answers in your file.

Ceremony Guide   CSOC

Nuptials And The Undoing & Parting of Ways Ceremony

"BESPOKE YOUR CEREMONY"

The Wedding Vows

Finally, will you share them with each other or keep them a secret until the wedding day?

Will you write them separately : Yes/No
Please circle and let the officiant know
or together: Yes/No

This is meant to be helpful to us and not to make you feel at all uncomfortable.
Your answers will be very helpful in preparing this ceremony.
Remember, to send them only back to us and let us know
We will save a copy of your answers in your file.

Decide how you want your vows to come across, agree on the format and tone with each other. One tip: "Include promises that are broad in scope, such as 'I promise to always support you,' as well as very specific to the two of you, like 'I promise to say "I love you" every night before bed,'"

Do you envision them as humorous?

Poetic and romantic?

Will they be completely different or will you make the same promises to each other as you would with traditional vows(you can do a little of each)?

We know some of the questions are intense and you do not have answer all of them.

3. Recital - a more personal vow, spoken from memory while looking directly into the partner's eyes, and without prompt by officiant. This format can be tricky, especially if the vows are long and complex. A written text (cheat sheet) tucked in a sleeve for backup is a good idea for this option. If yours are running longer than 3 minutes, makes some edits. Put some of the more personal thoughts in a letter or gift to your fiancé on the morning of your wedding and save any guest-related topics for your toasts.

The Family Celebrant & Officiant

"BESPOKE YOUR CEREMONY"

FOR ON LINE PAYMENT SIMPLY LOG INTO YOUR ONLINE BANKING AND CHOOSE interac-e-transfer
Recipient name is: _____ and e-mail: peerlessmoments@gmail.com
Type in the amount _____ and create a security question to give to
The above officiating minister and then confirm for the payment at
peerlessmoments@gmail.com ; Or by simply texting/calling ___-___-____

Upon accepting the payment you will receive receipt and will be deducted a fee of $1 from the bank for the service as extra cost. paypal.me/PeerlessMoments
Or visit paypal.me/PeerlessMoments

With **PayPal** you can also register for an account and from there I will send you a request of payment Followed by a receipt/invoice has been given
And will require your registration name and e-mail address account.

Credit cards may deduct an extra 2.9% + 30 cents maybe applicable

As these institutions/retailers provide invoice/receipt; please inform to the above Peerless Moments, as desired for an invoice too(these are flat rate prices and don't require any tax deductibles).

- NB: 50% Initial Deposit Fee is Payable before starting and with a 25% Non- Refundable.

- Final Agreed Invoice to be paid in full on the day of Ceremony and before the paperwork signing.

So let us get started

Chapter Four:

What are my Options?

As a Canadian Celebrant your service options that you offer must be simple to understand. Best number to go with is 3 and to highlight for example, as STANDARD_ TRADITIONAL_ BESPOKE. This book has its pointers for more encouraging results, you can also consult with your tutor. Although a bespoke ceremony might be misinterpreted; because of how it started off as (originally leaning toward the more elaborate), this does not have to be the case. We strongly recommend that you adapt much faster and to promote for all your ceremonies, as to be custom made.   Otherwise you will be looking at quantity, running off the same templates and with half the value. This can make the difference from a $150 standard ceremony to a $300 starting point one. In this case, why would a client choose this package, over a religious official's? Template run offs, also seem to have their way with, the more traditional packages as well. Again, why would anyone be interested in the same manner, of a $300 script and as they would be getting, from a church service and/or any other Celebrating Life provider/Ceremony service affiliates? Your options might start off as "Keep It Simple Stupid" and/or end up with "Keep It Simple Stupid". Either way, the only thing that will be of any real significance, is the value.

A Celebrating Life specialist, is not the title that we want to hold here. Rather every Canadian is welcomed, to join in; acting independently as members and with the freedom to identify authentically with our Canadian Society Of Celebrants fellowship. Helping to lead the way into a refreshing new system of bespoke contributors; that stimulate the publics imagination, to continually expand and uninhibitedly co-create with self-expression.

The Family Celebrant & Officiant
Nuptials And The Undoing & Parting of Ways Ceremony

Packages and Pricing

Now that we got the interpretation sorted, the 3 main categories can be as follows:

STANDARD_ TRADITIONAL_ ELABORATE

In this case clients can purchase a Standard; Traditional and/or Elaborate ceremony package (ensuring everything that they desire is included). All packages will have the exact requirements of a tailored ceremony script creation. What the packages contain might differ slightly; again left for your awareness of comfort to consider and reinterpret. The following is an example of what,

The pack can contain:

- A ceremony booklet; containing some modified ceremony templates (to select their preferred choice from a comprehensive selection), and several options of poems; readings and quotes.
- A ceremony choices guide and how to plan.
- An order form of their choices for their ceremony script creation.
- A presentation folder with a copy of the ceremony's "à la carte finale script de jour".
- Also can included an Order of ceremony and a commemorative ceremony certificate.

Normally a Celebrant will require at least 6 to 8 weeks before the actual date of the ceremony. When booking in your clients inform them of the bespoke ceremony timeframe requirements. Mandate at least 4 weeks prior to the event; to allow for the coming together of the script and for returning it back to them. This will allow enough space to plan their ceremony comfortably and make choices.

Chapter Four:

Packages and Pricing

The sample of the religious officials Ceremony package was a perfect example to included a price list and further explained the 3 options. It also is very clear that there is a 90 day window to perform the marriage legally. Your client in most cases has to be informed of just how much time will be required; because want the legal formality of a civil partnership or wedding might not apply in this case. Instead they might want to opt for something more non-conventional to mark their relationship, express their loving union, share their feelings with friends and family, or simply (chapter-two) have a quiet commitment ceremony for a few close witnesses to their relationship.

Your client may also want to interweave their ceremony with one or more of the "Special Ceremony Elements" provisions.

When asked to purchase items that clients want to keep after their ceremony; further costs must be agreed upon, such as: witness book, hand-fastenings, unity candles, coloured sand, order of service being printed, witness parchments and so on. It is a nice touch and can also provide you with a little extra income.

So this pretty much covers the essentials and to how it is the increase valued that a celebrant (with product and services)can bring. The basic cost of the ceremony can now be confidently rearranged: from $529.00 to over $1500 for clients with elaborate tastes. This includes home visit, telephone contact with you, a draft ceremony for checking, order of ceremony agreed, friendly support, liaison with their venue, walk through prior to ceremony, professional delivery of their ceremony in the venue of their choice(incurs an overnight stay or much travelling) and their own keepsake written copy of the ceremony.

The Family Celebrant & Officiant
Nuptials And The Undoing & Parting of Ways Ceremony
What is a consultation ?

☐ A safe space to discuss the kind of ceremony and focus solely on what the couple and family would like to have, for example: (standard)/traditional, Simply Divine and non-conventional, or a short and simple elopement(The Quicky) ceremony.

☐ A time set aside to go over all the possible components for the ceremony using whatever modalities you have come up with for structure, for example: The Interview Checklist And Questionnaire. As well as to get a feel for the couple on mutual preferences incorporate into the ceremony, for example: vow options, ring exchange options, music, readings etc.

☐ Inform clients, that as a Celebrant, you are not licensed under the Marriage Act, to perform the specific verbal legal ceremony. Make it clear to them, of their options and how it can co-operatively be adjusted; with the collaboration of a religious official. Otherwise this very short and brief ceremony, can take place, before hand and possibly at a later date. Perhaps that is all they are interested in; make certain that they are well informed and that you are not providing those requirements.
Make sure to advise them, that just because you cannot speak the mandatory declarations; that there is nothing that can hold them back from having a "*Commitment Ceremony*" before hand. The difference in having a ceremony before the legal ceremony is just that (a Commitment Ceremony Ch.Two).

Ceremony Guide   CSOC

Nuptials And The Undoing & Parting of Ways Ceremony

What is a consultation ?

☐ Explain how the intentional part of the ceremony can be engaged with physically and reached emotionally; when further explored with ritual and readings. This is where you highlight your personalization methods. The importance of a questionnaire and an interview checklist, is all about this consultation. After getting a feel of them and them of you; ask for a non-refundable cash deposit to confirm the booking's date and time. Keep in mind however, to also make room and be accepting of those couples, to whom prefer, not to go with any narratives.   After the consultation:

☐ Help them to facilitate with their selection of ceremony components. Encourage them to choose on their own favourite ceremony style. The theme can be anywhere from religious mixed culture, tropical, movie star and famous people impersonations, Medieval as well as, very simple and basic. Advise and guide them along the overwhelming task, of ceremony content.

☐ Bespoke scripts are all about modifications, adjusting and final tweaking. What is their story(how did they meet)? Allow some space for the clients to work out the details amongst themselves and then get back to you. This information will then be emailed back to the Celebrant. Be flexible for further add-ins and allow for the ceremony to reflect their personality; as a couple and the love they feel for each other.

The Family Celebrant & Officiant

Chapter Four:

Nuptials And The Undoing & Parting of Ways Ceremony

What is a consultation ?

☐ Note that all meetings for consultations can be accomplished live and interactively on line. Determine whether there is a need for a second consultation and/or during with the rehearsal. The second meeting can include a "talk-through rehearsal"; where the details and flow of the ceremony are confirmed. Reassure them of your professional willingness to cooperate with all other vendors and service/agent representative providers.

Before the consultation but not always the case:

☐ It is a good strategy to have as much covered with your clients online and well before any consultation.
The best planned out strategist uses their time effectively and efficiently. Especially now more than ever with the lock downs and Covid-19; it is to be expected that everything is done on line. In actual fact and for some, the day of rehearsal, is the only chance they really get; for an in person physical contact appearance.

☐ Once the clients and Celebrant have confirmed their agreed upon availability; the Celebrant can then, set up a date and time for an initial consultation.

Ceremony Guide   CSOC

Nuptials And The Undoing & Parting of Ways Ceremony

Some adaptable Script pointers And Content Order
The following sample headers can help to guide along any format and with its entitled particulars further; to expand upon and adapt to your very own Order of Ceremony, as well as, with The Anatomy of A Ceremony. Applicable starting points for commitment and/or vow renewal ceremonies too.
The content order can be altered at your discretion.

Meet & Greet
Admin
Please take a stand
Signal in Processional Music
Everybody sit
Begin from Script }- Welcome- Intro
Remembrance
Words on Marriage
Scene In / Reader 1
Element 1
The Story
Element 2
Vows
Ring Exchange
Announcement
The Kiss / Cue Applause
Element 3 / Parchment
Cue Music
Element 4
Giving Gratitude
Scene Out
Close
Announcement reiteration / Applause
Recessional Music

The Family Celebrant & Officiant
Some adaptable Script pointers And Content Order

It is always a good idea to colour code your script; have all of the reading poetry and any other quotes in green for example, your timing in red; Music/lyrics in blue; Anything that the Celebrant will say in black; Instructions in gray. Make note that these details are for you the Celebrant and not made visible to the client's copy. Although you can bring more value with colour to your clients script; the following are adjustments that you as the Officiating Celebrant can learn from.

Signal in Processional Music
Music Sysyphe - Handfasting (Magic Wedding)

Welcome, please be seated….. (0.30)

PAUSE 2,3,4

Good afternoon and welcome to this wonderful occasion for the right to celebrate the wedding ceremony of Janine Ervan and Bethany Coey.   (0.30)

Ease into your script's pace with a "PAUSE". Find your level of comfort with each section and how many lines before breaking for a pause,(maybe each section of the text of your script to 4 or 5 lines). The pace is the pulse of the scripts momentum; with every pause the audience can become more attentively grounded, with you and in with that moment.

PAUSE 1, 2,3
Learn to utilize the "PAUSE" method; because your audience can easily become distracted. Ideally between paragraphs; in and out of readings; announcements and all the other organized content headings.

Chapter Four:
Nuptials And The Undoing & Parting of Ways Ceremony

Some adaptable Script pointers And Content Order

PAUSE 1,2,3

Timing markers (0.00) are an asset within the synergy of a well synchronized script. Particularly when at a venue, where time constraints can be severe. This is a good habit to have! Double line paragraph spacing helps with the pace too.
Make sure to have a suitable font size for everyone and anyone; who wishes to easily pick up and substitute in, as the speaker. Just remember the Celebrant's script, is not the same as the client's script. Meaning that, it can become a public speaking product; that can go anywhere, from $100 and up to purchase. Eventually the Celebrant will adapt a consistent font(12-16)size and preferred(Arial, Calibri, Tahoma, Garamond and so on) similar format for all their ceremonies. With the right formatting and pace, each page can last, anywhere from 2 to 3 minutes, of reading(plus the final piece of music). This is how pricing can be better managed and for its value of a script, for example: a 5 to 6 page script can last for a 10 to 15 minute service and so on.
For the following script, the example given and during rehearsal came in, roughly at about, the 30minute mark. The invested time, to create a final script+The time it will take, to perform it = its value. In this case and at what point the ceremony becomes an elaborate service, will be left entirely up to your discretion.

PAUSE 2,3
Don't forget to utilize your headers and footers (they are not just for numbering your pages); always number your pages.

The Family Celebrant & Officiant

Anatomy of A Ceremony

START

Your Responsibilities On The Day	Responsibility of Others
Arrive at the venue an hour early - take 30 minutes to speak to the menu staff and greet everyone in. Find Emma Shake and Gertrude and receive the rings from them. I will start by taking the rings together in my hands for a moment of silence to visualize a blessing or two for them.	During this time; the ring warming ceremony will start off and finish upon the brides entrance, into the hall. Passing it along to the next; until all of us who want to make a wish or give a blessing for Janine and Bethany. The rings are passed along and finally end up again, in the hands of the best friend; of each and to then pass on for the couple, to place on around each other's finger, during the vows.
Q-processional music	Press Venue play Processional music
	Soon as they enter from opposite
- Welcome and Rose Ceremony	Sides that there are the 2 flower
	girls with the basket of petals
	2 girls for each to walk in front of them so to pave the way for
	them walking on a bed of pedals
	make sure they take shoes off
	Anna and Janice together with basket make their rounds; with red long stem roses. Bethany's mother (in loving memory) will be the empty seat and next to her grandmother. Mable will receive one of the two roses from Anna and while placing one on top of the empty seat beside her.
I read	
"Unconditional Love" by RmA	
introduction of Bethany & Janine's short story	
Q- for Bach air on the G string	
piano	the soloist pianist now starts to play

147

Ceremony Guide   CSOC

Anatomy of A Ceremony
Wedding Ceremony For Bethany Coey And Janine Ervan

The rings lastly come to me	Emma Shake has the rings to step up and give the first warming; then to each and every one of them
Hand-fastening ribbons, picked up by Celebrant. All ribbons pulled through; then cord pulled through and ribbons slipped off.	Assistants: Dennis and Emma Shake, help with and to tie the ribbons around the couple's hands, as the Celebrant speaks
Say ring Vows	**couple say vows & exchange rings**
Announcement: I announce the newlyweds 2nd Reading Apache Wedding Song/blessing	Both Bethany and Janine, will now make said promises to each other and with these words Bethany and Janine, both holding each other's ring; to place on each other, as they give their "I DO's" (one knuckle at a time). Newlyweds now Kiss
	* Parchment Signing to music
	During this intermission solo pianist will play on for roughly 15 minutes. Bach air on the G string piano solo, a new arrangement for solo piano created by Isisip
I make my last announcements	**Dennis** to play guitar and for guests to sing to Beatles song I want to Hold Your Hand
* Closing Words	
Q-Dennis	
	Everyone is singing
	Couple have the flower girls bring shoes and off they go.

FINISH

The Family Celebrant & Officiant

Celebrant Copy:

WEDDING CEREMONY DRAFT

FOR

JANINE ERVAN
&
BETHANY COEY

Wednesday, December 16, 2015

10:30am(EST)
Castello Beach Hotel
Mahe Island, Seychelles

Ceremony Guide   CSOC

WEDDING CEREMONY for Ervan, Janine & Bethany Coey

• **Processional Music**

Music Sysyphe - Handfasting(Magic Wedding)

During this time, the ring warming ceremony will start off and finish upon the brides entrance, into the hall. I will start by taking the rings together and in my hands for a moment of silence, to visualize a blessing or two for them. I will then pass it along to the next person and that person will do the same, passing it along to the next; until all of us, who want to make a wish, or give a blessing for, Janine and Bethany. The rings are passed along and finally end up, again in the hands of the best man and made of honour; to give to the couple to place on and around each other's finger, during their vows.

Entrance of the 2 brides and synchronized as they come down from opposite sides, to join together. They will enter to be greeted by the 2 flower girls each carrying with them their basket of petals. They will follow them down the isle and on each side, casting a path of petals for them to walk on; until they meet at the center and where a pile of petals are already there, for them to stand on.

PAUSE>>> Good afternoon and welcome to this wonderful occasion; to celebrate the wedding ceremony of Janine Ervan and Bethany Coey.

My name is _____ _____ and as a Family Celebrant it is a privilege to be asked by Bethany and Janine to conduct this ceremony. I am greatly honoured and to further extend, with my sincerest blessings, in this, their future endeavors, together as one.

30 sec.

Instructions   Celebrant   Readings   Timing

The Family Celebrant & Officiant

PAUSE>>> In the names of their remaining family together and with dearest friends. As you all have gathered here today, to help create a threshold of support; for the couple, to cross over and into their new life together.   **18 sec.**

PAUSE>>> Anna and Janice, together with basket, make their rounds with long stem red roses. Bethany's mother and in loving memory, we have reserved this empty seat, next to her grandmother. Once Mable will receive the two roses from Anna; she will keep one and place the other on top of the empty seat beside her. Janice is now presenting a red rose to Janine's mother, Natoli.

PAUSE>>> This moment we will turn to the mothers in recognition of the greatest praise Love and Gratitude to be given over their daughters hand in marriage. For putting up through all the many long years in looking after these beautiful grownups now indeed a miracle of love this token reminder with a rose we give them. Bethany and Janine, who are also offering this token of love to each other; in exchange are these red roses, made to each other.

PAUSE>>> I wish to now with this ceremony add this read called "Unconditional Love" by R.m.A

40 sec.

PAUSE>>> Celebrant:

We came from a world without knowing it had choice.

The path of Love, replaced a journey full of fear; it would be well to consider these conditions as symptoms of a dysfunctional civilization:

PAUSE>>> Celebrant:

Replicating from the one into the many of its dutiful oblivious distractions.

We were taught in the doing that we must struggle with resistance that constantly feels better when we are exploited by it.

We learn in the giving of compassion how resilient we have become from the conditional restrictions on who or what we can and cannot love.

PAUSE>>> Celebrant:

The Family Celebrant & Officiant

To comprehend the madness and in its effort,

to possess another's love;

As it is not ours to hoard, nor give away.

The time has finally come, where we must learn to be

And trust, in the deserving of this worth;

that we admire, with appreciation

By gracefully surrendering, into the earning of its gratitude.

This graceful momentum of our being;

moved unconditionally and in love, with each other.

We do not buy into this feeling, we simply just accept it.

Unfolding and from our very own consent,

intentionally we engage with it.

To study love, we must be touched by it.

To trust love, we must believe, that we are in love.

This feeling, is the very strength that guides and our confirming

truth by it. With unconditional dedication we trust in this faith,

As a vision of beauty, that is forever growing.

2:20 min.

PAUSE>>> As a student hairdresser from before and now a dearest friend of Bethany's. Alfred can recall, 3 years ago roughly; when the same gathering was present and as we all are here today, during his birthday party, when these two did meet.

PAUSE>>> Bethany was his teacher and now about to be married to one of his best client's and friend. In truth he was the matchmaker of this love, that was brought together, unknowingly and unintentionally. How funny things, they have a way and here maybe again, for some of us, this might be so. As true, as when these two did meet and here we are, in paradise; of all places, in the world to travel and this far, to be here today. A great opportunity, in so many ways and for all to share; even for the single members of this crowed, who have accepted in this visitation, to be here.   1 min.

PAUSE>>> the hand-fastening and then, into the ring/vows

PAUSE>>> I am certain that for the most of us here at this gathering have heard before the common saying "Tying the knot"?
Traditionally practiced and dating back to Celtic/Scottish tribes that gave it meaning of a year and a day as a proposal.
Amongst the Scottish villagers who had at the time this idea before the actual marriage ceremony and exchanging of any rings.

The Family Celebrant & Officiant

PAUSE>>> In today's world, it is favoured well within the Royal family; however as it was with the Celts and most common amongst the Wiccan's too. Traditionally it was meant to last as long and until the actual consummation. At this time the fastening I will slip off; however the knot from the cord and ribbons, can outlast forever.

PAUSE>>> Bethany and Janine, did not think of performing a betrothal and firstly at a separate time before.

3 years later, both are now wishing to undergo this experience; more so for the fun of it. Included into the ceremonial venue and remodeled to perform right now, for a very meaningful Handfasting version.

1:25 min.

Celebrant: picks up the Handfasting ribbons.

Assistants: Dennis and Emma Shake, help with the placing of the ribbons and around the couple's hands, as the Celebrant speaks.

PAUSE>>> With these ribbons and unity cord I bind the two, together from their wrists.

BETHANY And JANINE, DO YOU BOTH ACCEPT WHAT I AM ABOUT TO DO, IF SO, PLEASE RAISE BOTH YOUR WRISTS FORWARD WITH PALMS UP !   **20 sec.**

Red ribbon draped around couple's hands

PAUSE>>> With this red ribbon, of passion and will, I fasten the both; Bethany and Janine, joining your passion and will, into the one.

May the desires you have for each other, be always present; to bond within your blood and for each other always, to surge through you alike.

Blue ribbon draped around couple's hands   22 sec.

PAUSE>>> With this blue ribbon, I fasten Bethany's and Janine's sensitivity to each other; made fluid through emotional expression. In a blissful combination of the two and in surrender to each other's rejuvenating changes; always quenched forever more, from each other.   22 sec

Green ribbon draped around couple's hands

PAUSE>>> With this Green ribbon of stability I do fasten Bethany's and Janine's life; to ground with earthly pleasures of abundant nature's nurturing delights. To always be reminded of their connection to the earth and to each other's well being-ness; over and above, the material adorations of expression.   26 sec.

The Family Celebrant & Officiant

Yellow ribbon draped around couple's hands

With this Yellow ribbon, of communication, I do fasten Bethany's and Janine's mindfulness, for each other. To always listen to the whispers of each other's respectful knowledge and accept it humbly in each other's differences. May the both of you continually find the higher consciousness, with each and every breath together.

Inhale and exhale out connecting with this yellow ribbon.   30 sec.

Black cord draped around couple's hands

PAUSE>>> With this Black cord, let it be the source; from which all of nothingness, comes to be something.   10 sec.

White cord draped around couple's hands

PAUSE>>> With this White cord, is the final product of fruition, the manifested solid circumstantial and evident. The matter presented and made ready;to occupy space and with fact as entitled.   20 sec.

Red ribbon pulled through.

PAUSE>>> With this surge, you will ignite each other; into creative expression together. The will of this red ribbon, is that of you, as twin flames reunited into one. Now look into each other's eyes and see the ambers of this connection and in the physical co-operatively find always the sunny summer's day to prosper together with.   30 sec.

Blue ribbon pulled through.

PAUSE>>> With this Blue ribbon, be flexible always; open to each other and in the vastness of any conceivable parameters.

Your Souls refreshed within their taste as one eternally and that you both from this day forward share intuitively for each other.   20 sec.

Green ribbon pulled through.

PAUSE>>> From earth this emerald reminder and that your hearts be completed and connected. The giving support and touch of comfort for each other and when the silence of winter's chill appear. Experience this peace it generates, in the stillness and together grow the strength from it, for each other.   25 sec.

Yellow ribbon pulled through.

PAUSE>>> With this Yellow ribbon's intention to remind for newer and more fulfilling places; that the two will find together. Expanding into each other and unfolding gracefully, in every moment;excited for the joyous adventures, on your journey together.   25 sec.

Black cord pulled through.

PAUSE>>> With this Black cord be mesmerized, in mystery; this bond made from love, it is a must to stay open always, to receive it.
     20 sec.

The Family Celebrant & Officiant

White cord pulled through.

PAUSE>>> With this White cord will be of proof made many to reveal. The why and how in knowing the experience together; it is that of what miracles are made by, in bringing and keeping you happily ever after, together.

18 sec.

Celebrant takes the binding cord and says:

PAUSE>>> With this cord that I do bring to bind with and from a place of choice; for as long as the moment feels right for both and in this co-operative expression with each other.

15 sec.

PAUSE>>> Let this gathering be of witness and that this lovers' knot be truly tied; to establish them ready for their promises to each other.

15 sec.

Cord pulled through as ribbons slipped off.

PAUSE>>>

Both Bethany and Janine will now make said promises to each other with these words.

15 sec.

• **Vows/Rings**

Bethany Will Go First

PAUSE>>>

Bethany's: When I started thinking about my vows.

I decided that a good place to start, was to explain my love for you and on this endless list, I do include: your love, your kindness, your empathy, your creativity, your beauty and your amazing eyes.

Janine, I've been feeling this love with you, more and more every day; for the last 3 years and from when we first met, at Alfred's hairdressing social/Birthday Party. From there, it started very easily and tentatively; simply by the passing of these frequent messages and from the internet, for a good number of months.

PAUSE >> We had no idea how this could possibly be taken seriously; But from the very first moment I met you, I felt the electricity. I was defenseless against the instant rush of fascination and love for you.

PAUSE >> Janine, you are the most beautiful and kind person I've ever known; your impression continuously amazes me, who you are and how you see the world. You are my inspiration and my critic. My motivation and my reflection. You are my best friend, a true companion and a beautiful woman. I love you so much Janine and I can't wait for us to share the best of our lives together; because my world does not exist anymore without you in it.   2 min.

Instructions   Celebrant   Readings   Timing

The Family Celebrant & Officiant

PAUSE>>> Janine's Vows: "I DO" !

Here we are, free to choose unconditionally and with these vows, that we are making. The acceptance of this love, is inspirational and for both of us, in praise to each other. I give to you of me and say that "I am yours", I surrender in this trust that it is a mutually inspired interest my love, that brings us here today. I will support the many ways you are and choose to be; I believe in each other's spark, that which motivates our hearts in truth. Your thoughts I will encourage and promote as your coach and you as mine, in this happiness.

PAUSE >> With you included and for as long as we could ever stand it, to never part these ways, with each other. My faith in you, is the same I have in me and both we walk together. For as much as we can possibly endure this interest in each other I will be honoured. Through life's adversities I will be there holding your hand; this adventure is ours, to experience together. To us I say most graciously "I DO" my best friend and now my wife to be I say "I DO" Just like the many slivers that come together as one whole; I must say it to the many and as many times and yet this moment once is plenty. Oh my dearest Bethany ~ Yes I do !

2 min.

Instructions   Celebrant   Readings   Timing

Ceremony Guide CSOC

PAUSE>>> Bethany and Janine will now partake of the exchange of rings so that they may seal their love for each other in the sight of their gathered guests: you, honoured friends and beloved family.
20 sec.

Bethany and Janine, both holding each other's ring to place on each other as they give their "I DO's" (one knuckle at a time).

PAUSE>>> Do You Bethany and Janine choose each other as lovers and life long partners?   *10 sec.*

BETHANY'S/JANINE'S: ANSWER   *5 sec.*

Ring is held over first knuckle finger.

PAUSE>>> Will you appreciate, care for and praise each other, through good times and hard times?   *10 sec.*

BETHANY'S/JANINE'S: ANSWER   *5 sec.*

PAUSE>>> As soul mates to each other will you commit of yourselves in this likeness?   *10 sec.*

BETHANY'S/JANINE'S: ANSWER   *5 sec.*

Ring is held over second knuckle.

PAUSE>>> Will you both share of yourselves as a companion the support throughout; together for so as long as you both wish it to be this truth and most faithful of surrendered trust to each other ?   *15 sec.*

The Family Celebrant & Officiant

BETHANY'S/JANINE'S: ANSWER   5 sec.

Ring is pushed on.

PAUSE>>> With Bethany & Janine, as common law partners and having legally decided to change their names; it gives me the greatest of pleasure to be the first to introduce to you Wife' Bethany Ervan-Coey and Wife' Janine Coey-Ervan, to be partners in life.

PAUSE>>>

That was one of the loveliest experiences that we can all share with others.   25 sec.

• **Announcement**

PAUSE>>> Now with the first part seen as one of many facets to this ceremony we can and will forever more remember when looking at these ladies wearing these rings on each other's hand; for as long as they wish it so jointly blessed to continue on with this venue.

       25 sec.

• **2nd Reading**   **PAUSE>>>** As a final read I would like to share with all the "Pagan Wedding blessing,'" Take a look in your order of service booklet you will find it if you haven't already.

       15 sec.

Pagan Wedding blessing

Celebrant: Now the rain, will be of pleasure

As you provide each other shelter from the storm.

The cold, replaced by the warmth that you bring forth

from this day forward, for each other.

The longing for each other

replaced with companionship.

By Air you both be blessed, in wind and thought.

In this way too, the winds will bring to both much joy.

By Fire you both be blessed, of warmth and passion.

In this way too, the flames of love will fill your hearts.

By water you both be blessed, changing and flowing.

In this way too, a deeper love be yours.

By earth you both be blessed, reliable and grounded.

In this way too, supported with integrity and peace.

With enlightenment you both be blessed and grasp the unknowable.

In this way too, your souls be as one with the mystical to share.

By the Sun's rays be blessed and nurtured be your consciousness.

In this way too, a warmth to fill you both with joy and health.

The Family Celebrant & Officiant

Celebrant: Pagan Wedding blessing

By the blessing of the stars, distant and serene.

In this way too, the light will bring you both, guidance and tranquility.

Now you are two flames, but there is only one before you.

Be it the path of beauty that you both shall witness

In this way too, it will surround you both through all the years ahead.

Blessed be your days together and enduring the test of time.

PAUSE>>>

Janine and Bethany, Go now to your dwelling place to begin the days of your life together.

Blessed be your home and a place of happiness for all who enter it.

A place for growth and the sharing of expansion.

A place for melody and laughter.

A place of bliss and harmony.

Be blessed by your achievements with each passing day.

In praise and admiration eternally in each other's arms.

2:15 min.

Ceremony Guide   CSOC

• Parchment Signing with Music

PAUSE>>> let us take some time roughly about a 15 minute intermission; to sign the ceremonial parchment and for those wishing to gather and witness . .

15 sec.

During the intermission the solo pianist will play on for roughly 15 minutes. Bach air on the G string piano solo, a new arrangement for solo piano created by Isisip

• 3rd Element

PAUSE>>> We are back and without further a notice
Please have your container of bubbles; rice and/or any other symbols of joy ready to shower over them as they proceed out. Also for those of you who have the coconuts now is the time as the couple make their way through to smash them on the ground before them. Please make certain not to hit them so make it the timing all around their path as they walk away.   *30 sec.*

The Family Celebrant & Officiant

PAUSE>>> During this time, Bethany's brother Dennis; would like to play his acoustic guitar and for all who care to join in.

Please sing along to the Beatles song, I want to Hold Your Hand

15 sec.

- **Closing Words**

PAUSE>>> in closing I want to thank everyone here today for making this moment in time marked here to witness this couple now joined together in the bonds of love. 15 sec.

- **Recessional Music**

"I Want To Hold Your Hand"

The lyrics were removed for publication purposes

2 min.

Total Time: roughly 30 minutes

Instructions Celebrant Readings Timing

Chapter Four:

What are Conjugal Relationships?

Bethany and Janine had their names legally changed; because they are in a conjugal relationship. According to most provinces in Canada and in this case being Ontario; a joint declaration of a conjugal relationship outside marriage, is permitted (without a marriage licence). A "Declaration of Conjugal Relationship Outside Marriage", is an accepted permanence of a financial, socially and/or emotional and physical bond; it can and just like with divorce proceedings it too is subjugate, to the same legal and made applicable un-doings. The couple can only revoke a "Joint Declaration of Conjugal Relationship" by completing and sending to the Office of the Registrar General a Declaration(Form 4, Change of Name Act). There is no fee for this application and it is not exclusively made for "sexual relations" either; rather it indicates that there is a significant bond between the two as common-law partners. For more information, on how to change a last name to a spouse/ partner's last name; contact the office of your provincial governing body. The only thing we require to know here, is that it does not require a religious official.
The paperwork is between the couple to fill out, sign and mail it to the Deputy Registrar General to sign for their approval.

Things a Celebrant cannot say nor do:

* Cannot "Solemnly Declare the joining in matrimony" and "that of any lawful impediment". Nor to call upon any witnesses, in given affirmation; that the couple must voice out and for the purpose of a lawful intent, in their joining.

*Cannot Pronounce legally under the Marriage Act the couple; as they wish to be pronounced, for example: Wife and Wife. They can be entitled to these names; but not under the Marriage Act, to be declared as such. Be very careful when using these titles and on how you go about wording, the joining of the two.
It is always best to check these variables, with each province.

The Family Celebrant & Officiant

Nuptials And The Undoing & Parting of Ways Ceremony

Traditionally amongst Wiccans "Handfasting" is considered to be an ancient ritual, of commitment and love, between like-minded souls. It is a Nuptial of non-legal and/or legal natured ceremony. This type of a commitment can also be useful for civil ceremonies as well as leaning toward the more creatively accepting Spiritual ones. With the Wiccan custom side of it, to suggest a more elaborate and involved ceremony; than the above sample that was of Bethany and Janine. Also the order of which the rings and then hand fastening can also be rearranged to best fit to the clients liking. Their ties are not formed by these ribbons, or even by the knots connecting them; rather, they are formed instead, by their vows and soul pledge of their hearts bound together as one. As mentioned before, the tying of the knot around them in a figure eight symbolizes and on a more scientific level; the elecro-magnetism within each of us.

The holding of each other's elbows and as with the male and female component; of right(electrical) and the female as the left(magnetic). As they hold each other in place and with the forearms loose enough to drop; into holding hands after the binding and then they kiss(as the cords and ribbons make a figure eight around their wrists). As a reminder the ribbons and cords are not permanent and can eventually perish, whilst returning back to and through nature's elements. Where as their love that connects them in that moment is eternal. Just like Bethany's and Janine's ceremony; the Celebrant can modify, to add or subtract to from it as desired and to best tailor with couple's ritual of liking/beliefs. The couple may wish to incorporate and yet another aspect of the Wiccan custom; with the lighting of a unity candle. The Celebrant go on to invoke the rite of passage and with these few words: To ask by its divine light, the infinite to shine upon this union and offer a spiritual blessing to the ceremony.

The Celebrant can then begin to create a sacred and safe space with the casting of a circle, either out loud or in silence.

Chapter Four:

With Wiccan customs when the circle has been cast, a moment can be taken to consecrate the rings. Similar to a ring blessing by the guest and is perhaps where the idea had risen from.

A consecration is to ground the rings through elemental blessings either separately and/or during the casting of the circle. There is no right or wrong way and on the order of events; however religion is more righteous on the severity of each denomination and or following of certain tribal cultures.

As with Wiccan too, each tradition and as a the English language can be similar it too is subject to dialect variance.

The "Elemental Blessing" can be described as to explained from ancient times the communion with nature and her kingdom. With, "Air", "Fire", "Water", and "Earth", the couple, can be blessed and all who bear witness. That to abide with nature's elements can mirror the lessons for those participants responsible enough to accept each elemental as a gift. These attributes then can fully be expanded on what it is the elementals offer from their kingdom of awareness to our consciousness.

What we wish upon each other, are these blessings; in the formation of prayer perhaps, to resonate psychologically and from previous, past down experiences, as archetypal deities. "May their future be as bright, as the dawn on the horizon"; "Seeing not only with their eyes, may they together grow wise, with wisdom" and so on and so forth. "Father, Mother, Divine Spirit, we draw upon you here this evening; we feel your presence uniting in all in all things." "May you bless us and this couple before you in their union and those who have gathered here to celebrate in joy alongside with them". Then another actual blessing for the rings to be recited by the Celebrant and with the continual blessing of the couples union to each other.

The Family Celebrant & Officiant

Nuptials And The Undoing & Parting of Ways Ceremony

"Blessed be this marriage with the gifts from the East; may it reflect the resonance of both your Spirit's four bodies"(electric,etheric,physical,magnetic) and so on…

These four simple blessings can help them on their way and of their two paths, into one journey that begins now.

This can be a wonderful application and made very useful with other ritual tools and props combined; it can strengthen their energy levels forever in this love so richly deserving.

Then with the given promises/affirmations the rings are then placed on each other's finger and then the sharing of the vows(either or). After the vows are spoken the crossing of their hands over each other, and the cord then wraps around the couple, binding them together loosely and tying a knot.

Then the Celebrant, just like with Bethany and Janine's Ceremony continues to give meaning to the symbolizing and of each ribbons meaning and the cords. Couple kisses, the Celebrant unwraps cord without untying knot and hands it to the bride. The couple now jumps the broom. "Please turn to face your friends and family who love you. Ladies and gentlemen, I present to you _____"! The Circle is then taken down. The guests might be familiar; however it is important, that the Celebrant describes and gives meaning, to the ceremony context, for a complete and fulfilling experience. From the very beginning of what to expect, the circle: as the sacred space and a platform from which the couple, will feel safe to stand on. Perhaps it can be described, to resemble the "Chuppa"; a canopy that creates a sacred space, to stand under it. It can also be described and similar to the sacred womb, of Mother Marry. As the womb of mother nature, it is from where the two are born again, as one eternal. Where the couple can pledge unto one another; their higher selves and all that is divine, within them selves. In the Earth based traditions, it is considered the marriage, of the God and Goddess, from within.

A "Scripted Toast" (before/after the wedding sample):

A formal wedding reception can be held before the actual ceremony is to takes place. Traditionally, on the night before the morning church service and then the couple's elopement, can take place. Naturally, A Celebrant can replace the church service, with a meaningful celebration. Rather than having a stack of dreadful Q-cards; Why not opt to have, the Celebrant to add into the ceremony; or create a separate script exclusively for this occasion. The Celebrant can also be invited to these reception venues; that can be held during and/or after, the ceremony as well. When the reception is held after the ceremony the elopement normally takes place the very next day. There are no set standards of how the order of events must go and whether they will include the Celebrant. In the following sample, notice how this toast can be a great addition to the ceremony script.

<u>Father of the bride</u>: *There are certain moments in a man's life; that stay with him forever. Even when he grows old and demented. The summer of 1989 was one of them; it was the day I got married to Marg. The other was when she gave birth to my lovely daughter. Daisy it is hard to believe that I will be giving you away tomorrow.*
My dearest Daisy, you are my pride and joy. Tonight, is the last night I get to be, the number one man in your life. Scotty my boy, you better treat her well or have me to contend with. I stand here making a toast to the happy couple. May they be blessed enough to stand here someday; just like me and give a toast for my grandson granddaughter. With that said, I better give it up for Annie my mother.
She is looking very anxious for her turn.

The Family Celebrant & Officiant

Chapter Four:

Non-Religious Wedding Poems & Readings

Optional Readings & Poems

You are invited to select passages and poems, that best suit your hopes and goals. It is highly encouraged however, to also write your own; or have a family member or friend make a special statement.

How to express love within a marriage – by R.m.A:

Expressing the way we love another, is a giving experience; however not always accepted, by those who do not love us back in the same. The amount of give and take, determines the relationships and to the extent of this love. Small acts of kindness here and there, amounting to a great love habitually and by those who act upon it. To love means, that we care enough to know, when we are loved. We pardon those who wish to know love and never have felt it before. Maybe then the hurt will subside in them; in that they were never really alone and only but for this moment, to know it not in fear. To feel the joy it brings and surrounded in this happiness, that we are loved. Loved for ourselves, is the greatest accomplishment.

Love reflects love in return: The Divine Comedy by Dante

"The love of God, Unutterable and perfect, flows into a pure soul the way light rushes into a transparent object. The more love we receive, the more love we shine forth; so that, as we grow clear and open, the more complete the joy of loving is. And the more souls who resonate together, the greater the intensity of their love for, mirror like, each soul reflects the other."

Ceremony Guide   CSOC

Nuptials And The Undoing & Parting of Ways Ceremony

Non-Religious Wedding Poems & Readings

Reading from "A SEER"

"To love unconditionally, liberates us from the burden of that love. Expanding and receding our majestic souls magnetic as the ocean and mystifying. Side by side, so not to grow in each other's shadow. Together you stand, creating a sacred space and as pillars would, securing the temple of each other.
Love never subtracts from itself and does not have the need to add possessively to it; rather it is self sufficient by its own design. Love is a worthy connection and an unworthy disconnection, when we try to control its direction."

Spiritual Reading: A Hindu Love Poem

"Let me not to the marriage of true minds
Admit impediments. Love is not love
Which alters when it alteration finds,
Or bends with the remover to remove:
O no; it is an ever-fixed mark,
That looks on tempests, and is never shaken;
It is the star to every wandering bark,
Whose worth's unknown, although his height be taken.
Love's not Time's fool, though rosy lips and cheeks
Within his bending sickle's compass come;
Love alters not with his brief hours and weeks,
But bears it out even to the edge of doom.
If this be error and upon me proved,
I never writ, nor no man ever loved."

—William Shakespeare

The Family Celebrant & Officiant

Chapter Four:

Religious Readings: Corinthians 13:1-8;13(modified excerpt)

"When I speak, with human tongues and angelic, as well; but do not have love, I am a noisy gong, a clanging cymbal.
When I can have the gift of prophecy, and, with full knowledge, comprehend all mysteries; I then have faith and that only with love, can it be great enough, to move mountains.
"Love is patient; love is kind. Love is not jealous, it is not pompous, it is not inflated. Love is not rude, it does not seek its own interests, it is not quick-tempered; it does not brood over injury, it does not rejoice over wrongdoing but rejoices with the truth. It bears all things, believes all things, hopes all things, endures all things. Love never fails. Neither prophet nor prophesy can amount and are nothing without love; It knows all tongues, feels their meaningless knowledge and as being nothing, without love. For we know partially and we prophesy partially, but when the perfect comes, the partial will pass away. When I was young, I used to think, reason and talk immaturely; when I became an adult, I put aside these things. In this moment I am certain and that we see indistinctly, as in a mirror, but then, face to face.
At present I know partially; then I shall know fully, as I am fully known. So faith, hope, love remain, these three; but the greatest of these, is love."

A Non-Religious Break Up Reading

A Heart Felt Moment

When morning brings in showers and the evening comes to
wither. Circumstances can change, in many ways
but how we feel, from happy moments that we shared
are in these memories, forever unchanging.
author unknown

Nuptials And The Undoing & Parting of Ways Ceremony

The "Parting of Ways Ceremony", is a hand parting rite of passage and might suggest the loss of a loved one.
The exchange of emotional support and perhaps similar to a "Wake"? With a vigil, we share of well to do and very meaningful memories; that might have benefitted from our association to the departed. A social and most obviously theatrical, in its dramatics to promote; through activities, that can engage the party in creative self expression.
The same transitional displacement of its members and similar to its grieving process; the separation will require the couple to move forward and in this case, without each other as before. Some of these cultural expressions and throughout the ages, have adjusted to adapt and modify the similar proceedings; from a departed loved one, to a divorce and/or separation.
In this case, no one really dies; rather they just acknowledge, with a willingness and an open heart to split off, into a new phase of their lives, apart from each other. Where only one partner is ready to move on and the other is not; sometimes a personal ceremony can also be a very healing process for this individual.
The Order of proceedings, for a Parting Ceremony; however will not necessarily be the same, as a Parting of Ways and/or hand_parting ceremony. As mentioned in volume one; however let us take a slight briefing of a *Celebration of Life* proceeding order to sample: Entry music and/or caroling~Welcoming by Celebrant and introduction to eulogy~Reading and/or Prayer ~Moment of Silence and musical interlude to reflect~Poetry reading~participants ~Celebrantclosing/benediction ~Committal music Caroling~Closing/Departure music.
Creating a sense of closure that can help us to intentionally accept the completion of a relationship and publicly be given the opportunity to really say "goodbye".
This is what these ceremonies have in common.

The Family Celebrant & Officiant

Chapter Four:

It can become a very grounding experience; to help process through forgiveness and the support required, for a complete transformation. During this "undoing event", the couple can forgive each other; to be most grateful, in the sharing of time and that they were granted together, had not gone by, as wasted.

In older cultures, divorce was a lot less prominent, and marriage was more a legal property rights contract rather than based on love of the participants." In the Wiccan concept, when love ceases, a marriage can be dissolved without guilt or regrets. As witnessed in the previous Janine Ervan and Bethany Coey Ceremony draft; the couple pledges to remain together "as long as their love shall last". Although not entirely traditionally Wiccan it reflected the culture of their circle. During a traditional Wiccan betrothal the couple is given a chalice; that ties them symbolically. This was not mentioned but an alternative smashing of the coconuts was. Smashing of the coconuts, is(crushing a light-bulb and/or glass flute, under the "Huppah" paradox) a ritual modified from Hindu beliefs; it can also make for a great addition, to a "housewarming ceremony". Perhaps Bethany and Janine were given a chalice; but never had a ceremony prior to(that we know of). They had made the pledge and for as long as it could last. This can give them the opportunity and just like in Wicca; to end the relationship, without violating any vows. An open-ended approach continues on the path of unconditional love; the will to continue on as friends and beyond a separation, of this kind. After the legal ramifications have been explored and whatever other legal and/or binding contracts; the couple may even decide to continue living together. In most cases the hand-parting can take place before and or after any civil law agreements.

Ceremony Guide — CSOC

Nuptials And The Undoing & Parting of Ways Ceremony

It is Janine Ervan and Bethany Coey's wish today to have you all gathered as you once had, at Mahe Island, for their nuptials.
We are gathered here today, as a community of support and to see them through their Handparting. These ribbons are now cut and symbolize the severing of your nuptial vows to one another.
You each now hold half of these ribbons; they are to be placed in the iron cauldron for the Undoing part of the ceremony.
The experience that you shared with each other as one is no longer; the responsibility, is that of your own now and not for the other. By the taking back of your names, you both have made it very clear legally and now physically to finalize with, in the Parting Of Your Ways. By this ceremony here today and after, see it as a new beginning. We must respect and honour this love; rather than not to have loved at all and be loved by it. In witness here today, the threshold of a supportive group; to be there also when one door closes and the other opens, in separate from the other's way of view. This chapter of their lives must end now for a new one to begin. The pain and sorrow too must be realized and forgiven; take from this part of the story, only the lesson and in its wisdom you have gained. The following, is a decryption from Wiccan ceremony traditions: The actual ceremony can vary greatly; however the concept of smashing the chalice, is the standard. The intent can be as simple as to, symbolically dissolve it in this way; by scattering the pieces into a stream of water and/or to simply bury them. From these candles that we light, the red; then the black and from it the Cauldron to begin.

Janine Ervan: *Bethany Coey, I release you from our ties that bind and from the agreement we once had made, to each other.*
I ask of you to find it in your heart and forgive me; for any hurts I have caused you. I want you to know, that I completely forgive you and have accepted to move on. I only wish the same of you.

The Family Celebrant & Officiant

Chapter Four:

Then from the source(black) candle she lights a white one, for her new beginnings.

Celebrant: As we dissolve by fire all the sentimental relics the alchemy is in the release back to the source; for a new formation to behold and from the lighting of the white candle.
This clearing too we must release and from the sentimental ties; what has united them, with these two rings, will be undone, in the just as well.

Janine Ervan, may you become enlightened from this white candle. Take it with you as a reminder and only the good that has given you strength and shared achievements together.

Bethany Coey: *Janine Ervan, I hope this has strengthened you inwardly; as it has done so with me. I wish from this experience we both have shared together; to reinforce our positive attitudes and realize this truth through this darkest night of separation.*
I accept your forgiveness and hope it from all the darkness to lead me to the light from where I can begin a new direction.
I must forgive you in order for this to happen and I am relieved that you have and are able to forgive me in return. I hope that from this break in life's patter, it will bring me to a place called faith and from there the knowingness of that will transcend from believing it so. The believing in me, rather and not in us, any more.

Celebrant: Well said and as we go about the next initiation; to transmute the energy from and clear the rings.

The above presuppose excerpt, was from the previous shared Nuptial ceremony sample.

Ceremony Guide   CSOC

Nuptials And The Undoing & Parting of Ways Ceremony

There can be song, dance and other such emotional expressions added to the ceremony. It can also involve the couple's children. The cords and ribbons from the couple's hand-fastening must also be present. This is where an undoing and cutting off, of the knot can be performed. The Officiant, will welcome the participants and all guests in, with a reading/meditative visual song and dance. A circle(N/East, in Gaelic "deosil & widdershins" taken down) will be cast, to create a sacred space and an invocation can be made; to invite a certain archetype of lord and lady to attend.
In the case of Bethany and Janine, it was in the symbolic meanings of being tied together; now in the theme of the cutting and undoing of the ribbons and cords. Rather than the quadrant watchers/deities and other such Gods; invite all who were witness to their nuptial instead. This must be done through personal invitation cards and/or the way the guest were, exactly invited from before. The Celebrant can then publicly speak of this confirmation; to ask both of their intent.
The Celebrant announces to them and exactly as before: "You both made a pledge, not too long ago; that you both would share yourselves, as and as companions be provided, the support for one another". "TOGETHER, FOR SO AS LONG AS YOU BOTH WISH IT TO BE" so it was, the truth and until this moment". "Have you come here to agree upon the parting of your ways?" Do you both confirm and with it the undoing by this ceremony?" The Sharing of words by others and continue by spouses lessons learned. Then the officiating Celebrant can use the script from before, for the undoing; Or just simply use a bolline or scissors, to cut the cords and/or undue the ribbons.

The Family Celebrant & Officiant

Chapter Four:

The following, is a decryption, from Odyssean Wiccan traditions:

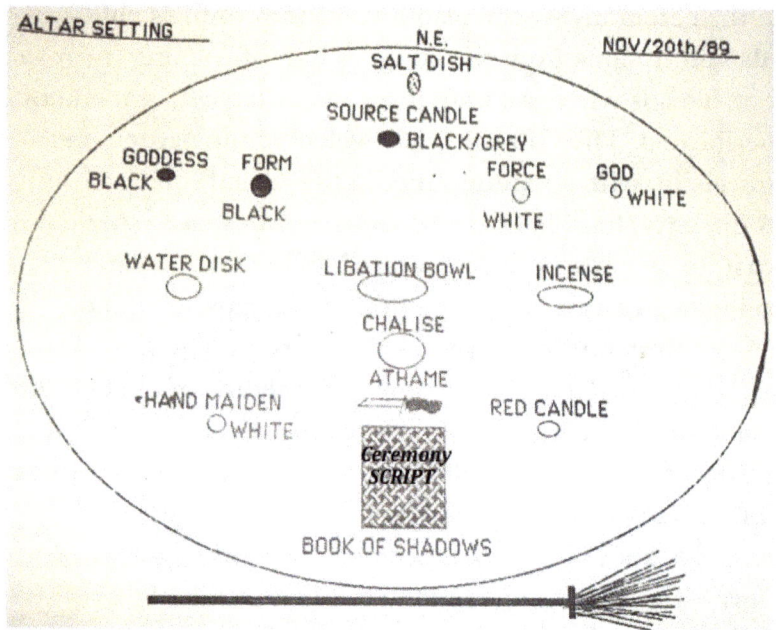

HERE'S
Another set up below, **whilst zooming in on all the details:**

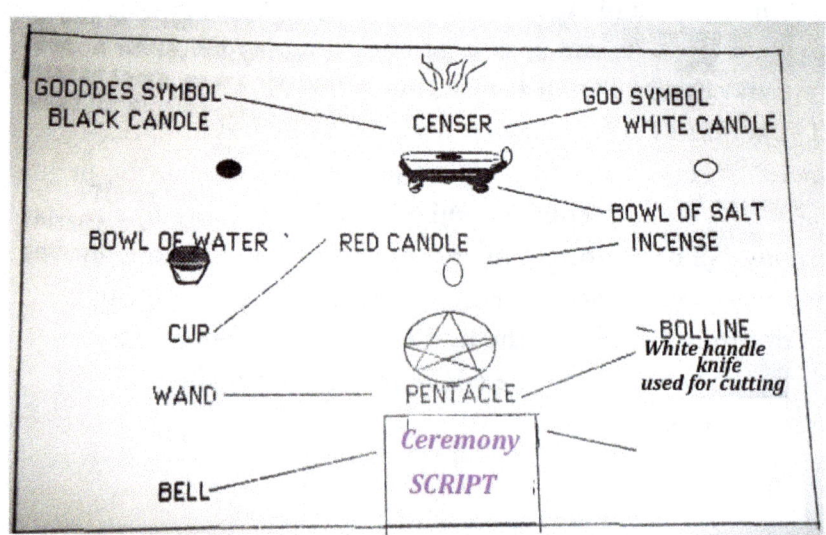

Ceremony Guide   CSOC

Nuptials And The Undoing & Parting of Ways Ceremony

The Altar, is a special table that can accommodate the capacity and to safely be equipped, as shown in the previous diagrams. Some sources have been known to recommend a cloth or something of meaningful significance; or colour to drape over this table. This book does not recommend such a notion; because that would be somewhat foolish, with the elementals of fire and incense. With Wiccan tradition, it is also a custom to jump the broom. In the following diagram below, you can opt to make your very own.

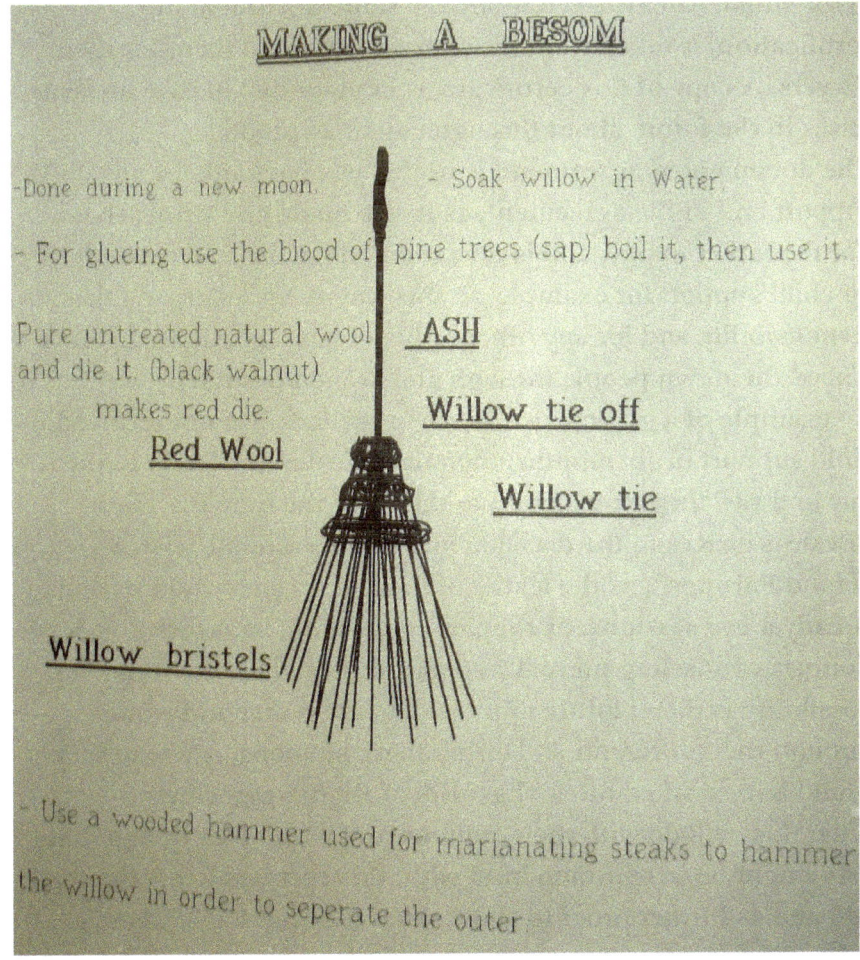

MAKING A BESOM

- Done during a new moon.
- Soak willow in Water.
- For glueing use the blood of pine trees (sap) boil it, then use it.

Pure untreated natural wool and die it. (black walnut) makes red die.

ASH
Willow tie off
Willow tie
Red Wool
Willow bristels

- Use a wooded hammer used for marianating steaks to hammer the willow in order to seperate the outer.

The Family Celebrant & Officiant

Chapter Four:

The following, is a decryption and from what can actually take place; within the Odyssean coven's sequence, of Wiccan events:

Before a hand parting is to take place; and especially when children are involved, an agreement must have been signed and witnessed, from the division of the couples properties.
In this alimony, where child support and what will happen regarding any children that they have; the agreement is placed on the altar and then the high-priestess and/or priest can go straight to the ritual. After the ceremony the same document of certification, is taken from the altar and given to them for their lawyers. A copy of this certificate, is kept on file; in case an issue arises in the future about this agreement as proof.
The documented agreement, is useful as a back up, for any child support and in the agreement, as it was made and witnessed;
For the father to pay, and is documented for the said amount as on child support for example. In this way the priesthood takes responsibility and for any other rights of passage, that they have placed their own people through and as a community.
An example of a go between, is when the lady has not received child support in six months; then the Priestess, will talk to the guy and say "hey, you agreed to this". By the time the High Priestess arrives to the decision and that the couple wish a "Hand Partings"; as the leader of their tribe, she would have had already a few sessions, of couples counseling, with them.
Couples counseling normally consist of, whether or not the possibility is there; for them to get back together and work through their differences. During these sessions, is where they would have worked out a "Last Bill of Right" agreement.
What they will do with their children and with other things that they might be in common bind with; this certified keepsake, can add and as further proof to show, what they have agreed on.

Nuptials And The Undoing & Parting of Ways Ceremony

The same witnesses(best man or bridesmaid), do not have to be there and to sign the certificate and/or the "Last Bill of Right". Normally the gathering is intimate and private with only but a few people; family and friends. The handparting/parting of ways and undoing ceremony; these can be separated and broken into segments. Weather permitting and to properly dispose of the previous artifacts; casted by the unity ceremony rights, during the betrothal and nuptials. When performed indoors, a circle around the altar, is cast. The same Gods that were called before; during the "Handfasting", are once again called upon.

The fragrance of the incense is prescribed as a "Parting Incense" and not the combination of herbs used for marriage.

The purpose for this, is to put a union together spiritually before the Gods and then the lawyers to give it the attention needed further. The priestess has a consultation before hand to prepare the couple; in terms of what they need to bring. The cord that they were bound with, the "chalice that they broke"; from which there is, a large cup and a small cup. With the broken cup and cord that they were tied with; their could be rings, as well as any other tokens and that they might have exchanged with(in a box). The priest and priestess will bless the smaller (cup)chalice and whilst they bless the big one. The couple drinks from their cup one last time and then it is broken; whilst keeping the (pottery/glass)pieces(in a bag), that represented the parts of their love and that no one else has any part of. The couple then take the larger chalice and distribute with bread to be shared by everyone(takes a sip and piece of bread).

The Priestess can talk(whilst sitting privately at the alter) to them about what they talked about before; and pertaining to the nuptial ceremony script. In this case where the counseling can also be explored from this discussion on the "Last Bill of Right" agreement to confirm and witness.

The Family Celebrant & Officiant

Chapter Four:

The following, is a decryption and from what can actually take place; within the Odyssean coven's sequence, of Wiccan events:

With those things brought to the "Undoing Ceremony" are then placed all by the altar All that is in that is written down already and in is doing that we take the cord and the cup and the ring and all that was there of their things from before that they buried and the earth takes it back and so then the couple is asked to whether or not they have come to an agreement about their disposition of things and what they have in the form of land and the custody of children and those other things of the mind that they need to address as to become separated.

That they remember the good things and the things that had brought them together in the first place and respect each other because of that. That they came together in the union of love but they no longer love in the same way and they no longer feel that way about each other. Things can change and that they come to part ways with today and we asked them to part in peace and not to part in any other way such as anger or other that may be harmful to each other. That they remember the good things and the things that had brought them together in the first place and to respect each other because of that. should not be speak ill of each other but simply agreed to be apart. That they came together in the union of love but they no longer love in the same way. They no longer feel that way about each other; because things can change and that they come to part with today and we asked them to part and peace and not to part in any other way such as anger or other that may be harmful to each other. Again this cord that once bound them together and now it is just a cord and with that they give it back into the earth and then this is the cup from once they drank down it with their private life time and now we give it back to the earth.

Nuptials And The Undoing & Parting of Ways Ceremony

A public speech can also be introduced; about how they came together with love and the sharing of friends in the community. The priestess could reword the script to better modify for this occasion further; "that things have changed and their love has changed". How "they no longer feel the same, about each other, as they did and have requested to part well on the way". "When the love is gone, it is better to move on; rather than to stay and live, in a negative space." "That they need to release each other and to recognize the friends they have in common." These friends must not be asked to take sides and/or separate them from these communities. "The love must not turn to hatred nor be reflected in this way by others; to simply just accept that they have agreed to be apart." The rings are consecrated, purified from the "Handfasting" blessing (undo and to unbind) and then given back to rightful owner; washing away the bonds of commitment and freeing the couple to enter into new relationships with others. Meaning the ring you have given, it is given back to you as you give the one back that was given to you and then it is given back to the earth. Ultimately the choice of what to do with the rings is entirely up to the individual. In this way the ring can still be worn; however the purification will have dissolved any previous energy held in place and from (by the other person that was wearing it) before them. The couple is then asked and based by the agreement that they had made before, to their Gods; to maintain within their community a certain manner of being and to clear them free of each other. The Priestess asks them to share the cup of friendship, as they once had shared it with love. The cup of love is provided by the temple from the Priestess; because the other was broken and returned to the earth. Then they go out and when they leave the circle, everybody goes with them.

The Family Celebrant & Officiant

Chapter Four:

To SUMMARIZE: "Handparting and/or Parting of Ways"

~ division of properties, paper that must be signed legal sits on the altar throughout the duration of the ritual.

~ couple comes in with witnesses and the circle is cast in the same way: call upon the same Gods, as with the handfasting (that was also kept on record of the dates of when it was done).

~ The cord they were and those things are then to be buried.

~ They are both in agreement publicly not so many people as in with the "handfasting" family and witnessing.

~ The incense is called "the parting of peace incense".

To swear by the agreement they have made by the Gods and to maintain within their community a cordial manner of being; that declares them free of each other. They share the cup of friendship; as they once shared the cup of love; leave the circle and circle is taken down and everybody goes.

Those gathered may be asked to socialize less than usual, as a sign of mourning. After this brief period, the circle is opened, symbolizing a return to ordinary time and space.

THE TAKE AWAY: From all the alchemical equations, energy is neither lost, nor gained; rather it can be transmuted.

As Celebrants we must not get lost in the indoctrination and/or level of secrecy required to preserve a culture's hierarchy and in what holds their tribes together. In this case the law of attraction has everything to do and with how Wicca operates in its given field of awareness. In more simpler terms, it is broken into an electro magnetic component. Meaning, the action and then the undoing of it, requires also the de-magnetism principle, of its energy; imposed and by our very own thought, that we believe to have imprinted. This is where the poles come in, of God and Goddess and that can easily be replaced with Jesus Christ and even Quan Yin; Mother Mary; Mary Magdalene; Sophia; St. John and so on.

Nuptials And The Undoing & Parting of Ways Ceremony

THE TAKE AWAY:
The use of Ascended Masters for consecration, to the casting of a circle. The quadrants can be Arch angel Michael for the South; Raphael for the East; Uriel/Auriella for the North (their genders can fluctuate); to Gabriel/la for the West. A good listener becomes the oracle and as the Celebrant you can help in tone to Officiate the message of your clients intent; what best resonates to imagine and then create. Remember the ceremony is in reference to the undoing and parting of ways; perhaps the previous ceremony might not have been scripted and/or officiated by you and that is okay too. When we are dealing with the psychology and personality of our clients, we must take these(that make up for the ceremony) activities into consideration. Perhaps we can break the elementals further, into sub-personalities. What is it, that we can receive from the South and build on our inner wisdom. What is it, that we can take from the West, to heal our emotions and from it, the energy to develop it from imagination; the images(s) we can use for personal growth and self expression. How we can then come home into the one, from the nurturer of the North; that we can find from within ourselves, this stable nature. It is from the heart that we can find our center and reclaim our magnetism. That brings us to the East and from our solar plexus the warrior, brilliant and yet protective with boundaries. A First Nations Native Smudging can also make for a wonderful cleanse and consecration. Perhaps your client has some resonance to a certain tribe such as the Canadian Cree and/or American Cherokee and that can vary. A medicine wheel can consist of: For example, the burning of sweet grass and the colour red in the North; the offering of tobacco(on a gold/yellow plate)for the East; the burning of cedar in the South(on a white plate) and Sage in the West.
"As above, So below And from within_Out."

The Family Celebrant & Officiant

Chapter Four:

Ritual Tools/Seals/Sigils Symbolic Emblems:

In the previous pages, there were a few diagrams, on Altar set up and how to create your very own Besom(broom).

ALTAR SETTING

THE SWORD

It is a tool in which causes change, therefore it is commonly linked with the element of Fire. Its phallic nature links it with the God. Its symbol of the Gods and power. An act of energy used to cast the circle. It's also set at the right of the circle.

THE BROOM (BESOM)

It is sacred to both the Goddess and God. The construction is more masculine than feminine. Yet, since it is a purifier, the broom is linked with the element of Water. This makes it passive in its nature and therefore symbolic of the Goddess. Then too, probably because of its phallic shape, the broom became a powerful tool against curses and practitioners of evil magic.

The ritual begins by sweeping the area lightly with the beson. The broom's bristles needn't touch the ground. While brushing, you visualize that the broom is sweeping out the astral buildup that occurs where humans live. This purifies the area to allow smoother ritual workings. In general, the broom is a purificatory and protective instrument, used to ritually cleanse the area for magic.

During handfastings the broom is often included. The couple to be married often ritually jump a broomstick to solemnize their union.

CAULDRON

Its a symbol of the Goddess, the manifested essence of femininity and fertility. It is also symbolic of the element of Water, re-incarnation, immortality and inspiration. During spring rites it is sometimes filled with fresh water and flowers; during winter a fire maybe kindled within the cauldron to represent the returning heat and light of the Sun. So it can be a focal point of ritual. It can be used as an instrument of scrying(gazing). It can also serve as a container in which to brew up Apple cider. Ideally, the cauldron should be of iron, resting on three legs, with its opening smaller than its widest part.

The cauldron can also be used for transmuting energy; through fire to burn away, hand-fastening ribbons and other relics, back to source. Perhaps the vows can be considered and from the paper they were written on; along with the nuptial ceremony script.

Ceremony Guide   CSOC

Nuptials And The Undoing & Parting of Ways Ceremony

Ritual Tools/Seals/Sigils Symbolic Emblems:

In the previous altar setting diagrams, a sword was nowhere to be found(improvise); however the athame and/or wand, can also do very well and with a besom, to replace its application altogether.

ALTAR SETTING
Tools

CHALICE

Symbolicly represts the womb in a more direct sence. Fertility and Possibility. It's used to pass around for wine blessings. The chalice can be made of nearly any substance: silver, brass, gold, soapstone, alabaster, crystal and other materials.

ATHAME

It's a tool that causes change, and is commonly linked with the element of Fire. It's phallic nature links it with the God. Its ment to project chanels of energy. Used primarely in the calling of the quarters. It's also used in wine blessing.

WAND

It is an instrument of invocation. It is also sometimes used to direct energy, to draw magical symbols on the ground. It is used in the same manner as the athame. It can also be used as a substitute for a sword. It is considered to be a Fire or an Air element.

THE CENSER "Thurible"

A Thurible is the container for the incense. It's symbolic of the element Air and the God. It also represents the East.

THE FIRE CANDLE

This is red and is symbolic of God. It represents the South quadrant and is the element of Fire.

THE WATER DISH

This holds water and is used to cleanse the area called when bringing forth the West quadrant. It represents the West and is the element of Water.

The Family Celebrant & Officiant
Chapter Four:

Ritual Tools/Seals/Sigils Symbolic Emblems:

ALTAR SETTING   1989/NOV/20

SALT DISH (Earth dish)
Contains salt.
Symbolic of stability and the element Earth.
Its symbolic of the Goddess.
- It represents the North.

LIBATION BOWL
Is a stopping place to make offerings to the Gods.
This is done by placing a small portion of your meal or even some wine and putting it into the libation.
It is symbolic of the Goddess and therefore feminine.

EARTH PLATE (CAKE DISH)
Is used for brushing Earth stones.
Used for cookies.
Its placed on the centre of the altar.

SOURCE CANDLE
Represents the beginning of the universe.
Its colour can be grey or silver preferably black.
It is the first to be lit.

BELL
It is a male symbol and is often used to invoke the God.
It is also rung to ward off evil spells and spirits;
to halt storms, or evoke good energies.
It is also used durring Samhain to bring the spirits forth from the other side.

Ritual Tools/Seals/Sigils Symbolic Emblems

As mentioned before and with the besom as being part of the unity ceremony element; rather than jumping the broom together, have the couple jump separately from each other. Symbolically this act will indicate that from here on their co-creating as before, is no longer. As in the case of Priest and Priestess performing these initiations; the Celebrant does not require their male or female counterpart. Normally the betrothal and the nuptials can be somewhat of an elaborate ceremony; however each segment and just like any other celebration, it does not have to be. The anointing of a fragrance alchemy oil, will also differ and made specifically for the parting of their ways. Initiating their forehead, heart, wrists, ankles and back home as single again. The oil can be a dotted-dab and/or exactly like the quarters, to form a pentagram/cross; or six and even seven pointed star. In this case, it does not have to be a ranking order formality, as it would with religious occults.

The sigil and or symbol can be most interestingly affective and very effective too. When using a Christian cross, it not only symbolizes resurrection; it is also very helpful in casting a sacred space and exactly as a Pentacle and/or Merkabah.

Again when drawing down the quarters, use your imagination to explore. One could draw from the NorthWest and in the same as the NorthEast together; from these points of reference and then go clockwise and or counterclockwise. In Australia and depending on the magnetic direction of the poles, a circle is cast counterclockwise and then taken down clockwise.

Casting a sacred space can be done, also with a cross and starting from the South, there is no real order and unless you choose to incorporate one; for example, the Egyptian ancient scriptures and perhaps from the Golden dawn. When anointing with the cross, it helps(ascension) to join the lower with the higher and from the solar plexus, to the forehead.

Chapter Four:

Ritual Tools/Seals/Sigils Symbolic Emblems

These are all spiritual expressions, from the collective's oversoul; captured into symbols and as emblems, to create religious factions with. It was never really designed to enslave people and with its limitations to exclude. As Celebrants, we are not interested in the suffering of these concerns; nor to become recognized from it and those things. We are inclusive in our practices, to please our clients and families, that come to us.

Invocations:

We do not have to learn through suffering, when we become awakened and to our very own existence. The less resistant we can be; the less the conflicts, that we will have to integrate. Invocation, is a form of channeling and we do this by tapping in to our and/or others psyche. The various archetypes, sub-personalities and just like Jesus Christ; these entities can become the mediums, between us and the higher self/infinite and divine potential. The practitioner of meditation will find the way, into a trancelike state and where faith resides most real. In this state, even the discipline of remote viewing, can become an achievable possibility(Edgar Cayce). We never question and/or doubt when on this level; because when we try to analyze, we will come right back out of it. In this hypnotic state we can become omniscient and this ideally, is how we can focus to invoke, the essence of a presence and/or intent.

Nuptials And The Undoing & Parting of Ways Ceremony

Initiations and psychological impacts:

Throughout people's lives and that which we all go through together and/or alone to experience. The imprints on our psyche's mind and the way we interact; whether they be personal initiations and regardless of having to belong to anything, outside of ourselves. These traumas can be lessons, that we can learn from; to share this responsibility with others, can make it easier. The grief that we experience and when we go through transitions, such as a divorce. Others might have experienced similar, but not exactly in the same way. The sharing of these experiences, can help collectively, with social evolution and personal growth. Psychologically, they shape our character; it changes our identity, or strengthens it, even more.

How our perspectives change, from emotional trauma and even physical; these are initiations and that can imprint upon us, in how we perceive the world. How we relate to others subconsciously, consciously and even unconsciously; this will have a lot to say about our interactions with society; the families we serve, their activities of interest and the Celebrant that they will relate best to engage with. These initiations become the adhesive, that holds in place communities and through societal conditioning, the families we serve. The influence is the imprinting on our world; that then intern imprints back on us.

We all can relate to having experienced difficulties and changes in our lives. Although it can be very convincing that a divorce ceremony can be a valuable healing start; it mustn't become an imposition. source of healing during this major life transition.

As the Celebrant, you might be able to organize a referral.
To consult with other such professional providers and that would include the qualifications of a licenced minister/religious official.

The Family Celebrant & Officiant

Chapter Four:

Nuptials And The Undoing & Parting of Ways Ceremony

Every experience has significance and deserves to be celebrated well. With a divorce ceremony, the couple must come to terms with all their attachments; to each other and that would include a grieving process. The sentimental factors and that of hurt and pain. This will include the close and intimate network of folk; the ceremony can help by bringing them together.
With friends and family to help reconcile the past; to support and encourage the persons to move forward and through the healing process of empowerment. The ceremony can assist the coping of any feelings of abandonment: with prose, poetry, music and other meaningful symbols. The ceremony will commence and as single lives, the journey to recovery in peace and happiness.
In the spirit of acceptance, participants within the gathering who have had indirect and/or directly experience of a divorce; perhaps can share their stories and to bring a broader impact of compassion, to the ceremony. The ceremony can involve them and within the space, to help the couple; to individually become motivated, with renewed commitments. Perhaps writing down and into a new chapter of one's book, called life; to welcome with fulfillment the dawning of new perspectives.
Transitioning through the co-dependency of having to survive another day; to living another day to thrive.
The compromise is over and the creative self has outgrown this self expression; from the victim it once knew, to the victor.
The Celebrant's mission is only to focus on creating a ceremony; to reflect on the families values, beliefs, cultural background, religious or non-religious. The couple, must have complete choice of and give the final approval over the ceremony.

Ceremony Guide   CSOC

Nuptials And The Undoing & Parting of Ways Ceremony

<u>What A(legal)SEPARATION AGREEMENT might look like:</u>

This Joint Agreement on this day _____of_____,_____   And
for the purpose of Separation

BETWEEN:

            _____
                in the Province of_____
            AND

            _____
                in the Province of_____

BACKGROUND information:
_____ and_____ were lawfully married on <u>month, day and year</u> and in the region of_____, Ontario. Unforeseen irreconcilable differences between them have caused them to agree to part ways and live as separate from each other; Subject to the terms, conditions and of the following documented contractual agreement. Within the said "<u>Last Bill of Rights</u>" made by fair accuracy, all financial matters reflected and for a complete transparency, to disclose, as per these pages of paper. Each member has consulted with an attorney; in relevance to their legal rights, arising from their legal obligation, as a couple and under the terms of this "<u>Last Bill of Rights</u>" Agreement.

The intention of this agreement is to address matters and under the said terms. Both parties are aware that this is not a final disposition; rather to help proceed with the duly incorporated and final outcome of a divorce.

Chapter Four:

What A(legal) SEPARATION AGREEMENT might look like:

IN REASONABLE RELAVANCE to the pursuant mutual conditional Agreement; that the both have entered voluntarily, to confirm that they be of sound mind and health.

To have promised the following reasonable requests and valued; in consideration to receive and within the sufficiency to what comes next that both bodies here today before me do acknowledge.

LIVING APART FROM EACH OTHER AS SEPARATE

Neither persons shall invite themselves unannounced and to be in the same living space and/or work place as the other.
Have agreed to live at least 100 meters apart; in a separate space and/or place from each other and have been doing so since Month/Day/year.

CHILDREN

There are presently three children born to this marriage.
The two eldest son and daughter are over the age of majority; as adults they are self-supported and emancipated.
The adopted daughter requires the care of her mother and her father has agreed the financial support; as per the $1000 a month on alimony and a joint custody there of. Both parties are in Agreement and that when she is old enough to live with her father; a minimum of a six night sleep over and within each month and/or school break granted. A leniency for a longer stay, must be agreed upon by both parties. When the infant is old enough and there should be proof of no coercion; custody amended further and can be reinstated upon said day.

Ceremony Guide   CSOC

Nuptials And The Undoing & Parting of Ways Ceremony

What A(legal)SEPARATION AGREEMENT might look like:

ALIMONY

A reasonable spousal maintenance, is made applicable in the amount of 25% child/preteen support; however an agreed amount of toddler's substantial and for its infancy of 50% per month from father's income; until she becomes of age, to be reconsidered for the 1.5% or 2% rate and/or none applicable reinstated as to amend upon that said term for re-evaluation.

ASSETS

The parties agree upon the house be handed over to the full ownership of the wife and toddler. When the child becomes of age, she will have inherited 50% of its deed and that would otherwise have been the entitled portion of her father's and/or husband from this said separation of marriage. Neither makes claims and/or obligation to any other assets and or possessions.

DEBTS

The parties agree that any previous secured indebtedness against, or attributed jointly must be resolved and equally made applicable until so.

Any indebtedness secured against, after the legal separation and pertaining to any items of property that either party is receiving under this agreement; will cease of any further joint credit debt and will be the sole responsibility of the party and/or parties of those particulars possessions.

The Family Celebrant & Officiant

Chapter Four:
What A(legal)SEPARATION AGREEMENT might look like:

GENERAL PROVISIONS
* Both parties will sign and give to the other right away; necessary documents of this agreement, that will take effect and to these terms.
* This agreement from both parties and about their relationship to each other; will replace any prior written and/or oral made agreements between them.
* Any portion of this agreement that becomes held liable for invalidation by a court of law; the unenforceable, or void part will be subject to amend and/or be further reduced to its extent and/or stricken out entirely as necessary to validate its jurisdiction of authorized enforcement.
* In the event of a dispute regarding from the arising circumstances by this agreement; both parties must seek professional advice or thereby counseling to help with the resolve prior to initiating a court action.
* Both parties can seek out from their mediation negotiations agree to provide and execute further the documentation and backup supporting letter(s) to help satisfy and certify thereby any terms per this agreement.
* This agreement can only be amended and in compliance through a legal entity and their given approved advice.
* As their fiduciary duty both parties have agreed on these terms in good faith and fairness toward each other regarding all aspects of this agreement.
* That the headings and/or any other be inscribed; because of convenience to be altered; removed and/or inserted.

Ceremony Guide   CSOC

Nuptials And The Undoing & Parting of Ways Ceremony
What A(legal) SEPARATION AGREEMENT might look like:

GENERAL PROVISIONS

* Unless invoked by in writing to reconcile this agreement remain in effect and to help ensure to the benefit of both parties; executrix, administrators and all other heirs to assign.
* Not withstanding however to the foregoing passage of years from either party; that both none the less of these intentions be bound and strictly by these terms from this agreement. Thereby the province of _____ will govern the interpretation of this agreement; the status of ownership and further divided or non divided and set wishes of property, between both parties and wherever either or both, may decide from time to time reside.

SIGNED by_____
In the presence of:

                                                _____
                                                _____

_____
WITNESS

SIGNED by_____
In the presence of:

                                                _____
                                                _____

_____
WITNESS   _____

_____
WITNESS

The Family Celebrant & Officiant

Chapter Four:

CERTIFICATION Of ACKNOWLEDGEMENT

I, Barrister and Solicitor_____

                                                   CERTIFY

Within The Province Of _____

On this day of _____ came before me, _____,

Whose name to the foregoing Separation Of Agreement and so acknowledged by signature on this Separation Agreement _____ and to have entered into this Separation Agreement by her/his own free will and volition, without coercion by any Party.

                                                _____

                                                Barrister and Solicitor

I, Barrister and Solicitor_____

                                                     CERTIFY

Within The Province Of _____

On this day of _____ came before me, _____,

Whose name to the foregoing Separation Of Agreement and so acknowledged by signature on this Separation Agreement _____ and to have entered into this Separation Agreement by her/his own free will and volition, without coercion by any Party.

                                                _____

                                                Barrister and Solicitor

Ceremony Guide　　　　　　　　　　　　　　　　　　CSOC

Nuptials And The Undoing & Parting of Ways Ceremony

After and/or before the undoing ceremony and the hand-parting the couple can and by Canadian law to remarry after a divorce. When an official certificate of divorce, is presented as proof; from the original or a court-certified copy of the final decree and judgment, a couple can then apply for a marriage licence.

A signed statement of sole responsibility: for each divorce (signed by both people who are planning to get married and a witness) legal opinion letter: from a lawyer of said province, addressed to both people who plan to get married, giving reasons why the divorce or annulment should be recognized in that province as a divorce decree or annulment: an original or court-certified copy in English or French.

A divorce outside of Canada, will also require a legitimate document of proof and by their law of the land jurisdictions. A translated and sworn in affidavit copy of the decree.

Completed Foreign Divorce Authorizations are sent to applicants by courier. To their full mailing address and as on the marriage licence application form, to then be delivered and returned to the provincial Registrar General's office.

This is not the Celebrant's concern; however the above given information, is our threshold and in the knowing very well, our boundaries. With the building of our confidence and know how; our clientele can broaden immensely, in offering these types of services and products. The legality of formalities helps us to not only better grasp, certain aspects of intent; it also qualifies with the Bill Of Rights certificate scenario and the signing of the Alimony papers, on the Wiccan Altar. Leaving from this chapter and leading us onward to the very next; with less confusion and hopefully more clarity than before.

The Family Celebrant & Officiant

Chapter Four:
Nuptials And The Undoing & Parting of Ways Ceremony

In Summary: A break-up can entail, a certain level of grief and that sometimes can be even more severe, on having an emotional impact; than that of, the losing of a loved one, from a death. Grief is a cluster of emotions and that must be allowed to process. Providing a ceremony, can be very helpful to the mind and that requires to accept closure. Divorce and like any other loss, they are all uniquely different; so too it will affect everybody, somewhat in its variation. The finalizing with the legal signing and court procedures aren't as scary when disclosed and made transparent and as this read has provided for this reason.

Also a relationship is not always legally declared, pronounced and documented. Performing a ritual can be documented as a script and later in the same way as before undone.

The "Undoing" and "Parting of Ways" is an important right of passage; that can help begin the healing process.

Just the same it mentally prepares us to move on from even a love affair and/or special friendship. It is as important, if not more; than the legal dissolution, intended to resolve with its issues and tying up loose ends. The Ceremony can involve both parties, children, family and friends, all in one; Or broken up, into two distinctly different ones (for one partner and than the other, on a different time and place). Every situation is processed from the heart uniquely and for this reason the ceremony does not have to involve both parties. By carefully deciding what best suits your client's situation; as Celebrants we must be accepting and open to all possibilities. It is significantly easier, to have both parties participate; however not all relationships break up synergistically and mentally synchronized. Forgiveness requires a certain release of the past and this can be achievable in the celebrating of it. The Funeral Officiant & Ceremony~ACIFC, volume one; to further help and provide, for more information.

Chapter Five ~ Renewal of Vows ceremony

PERFECT LOVE & PERFECT TRUST:
This term, will be made reference to often, in these cases and in the past scenarios, of all and/or any given loving event.
With very little explanation, it goes without saying; at its very presuppose and to suggest (a level of maturity)such a thing, as "unconditional love". Especially in the way of a "Renewal of Vows" ceremony. The promises and expectations from these conditions, predisposes the thought of *"unconditional love"*, to a conundrum of its paradox. The word committed relationships is an ideal example of this pervious imperfection. Could it be that the paradox in place was intended with the purpose to disclose about perfection, and the expecting and accepting of the human frailty. It is obvious then that the couple can accept to expect the flaws and on occasion the mood swings that accompany a lesson or two, for growth and expansion to consider. The unexpected circumstance, must be given space to recon with, to test out; because of any other expectations and that might have brought, them about in the first place. To be mature enough to allow forgiveness and as it is already known the same with in their hearts of hearts between them; is the strength of love, affection and friendship. To trust in the reason of their union and the vows they pledge; are not intended to pain the other with and over pettiness of further malice or ill will. The trust is in the surrendering fully and without an ounce of any doubt to give reasonable proof otherwise as to resist the other with these commitments and made from a place of unconditional sustainable love. To be divinely inspired from each other, together in love and without any fear of abandonment.
To live without the pressure, of any real expectations from each other and be able to securely feel, the sense of certainty, from trust, is the greatest and most perfect love there is.

The Family Celebrant & Officiant

What better place to introduce the concept of "Perfect Love and Perfect Trust", but in this chapter.

Vow renewals are a celebration of an ongoing love and a couple's commitment, to one another. In actual fact the level of maturity and in most cases, it has been reached; to fully digest these pledges, from a state of being and that can truly grasp to feel it, from a place of "*Unconditional Love*". It could very well be, that both can recognize, that the relationship has evolved; into something, altogether new and wish to mark that transformation. Maybe the couple might be getting maturely romantic and sentimental, in their later years; to revisit those vows, and that were exchanged, on their wedding day. As there is no legal significance for vow renewals, they can be as creative as you like. By accepting both the good and bad already; the couple has reached a stage in their life of a refreshing. One chapter closes and the next one begins, a new.

With a "<u>Renewal of Vows ceremony</u>":

* it can be a wonderful time to revisit the previous and from a couple's wedding vows; to realign them again with what best resonates and redefines their bond for one another.

* To redefine these modifications, within the changes, of the family unit, in effect and by sharing with them this special event.

* This time around it can add to the witnessing of the family and friends; that otherwise could not have been there previously and to accept those, that have dropped out from before.

* Reconnecting with the inner circle of their tribe and old friends; to return to the location of significance. An alumnus of revolutionary honour and with those guests, during the wedding ceremony so long ago; to amend and reveal the evolutionary truth, in the occasion, with a new community.

Chapter Five ~ Renewal of Vows ceremony

PERFECT LOVE & PERFECT TRUST:
In honouring this affirmation; that has been specifically designed to introduce and for any ceremony of this nature.
The Wiccan custom and as mentioned in previous, it must be in this chapter too, very well considered. The Renewal of Vows, are at the focal point, in Wicca and where it might not be anywhere else; as in the case of Christian(Greek)Orthodox.
Once the instructions are given to the couple; in terms of what they want to leave behind, they can then enter into a new stage in their life. The ceremony is about accepting the new version of each other and this changes their life completely.
To indicate in how they are going to deal with this; the Celebrant can ask to confirm and each give the rings, to be blessed over again. These rings as once have joined them before, have now a newer meaning and intent; for the purpose of rebinding and rather as a reminder, of the refreshing new partnership.
The Vows are generally written by the couple and modified from as before. In Wicca, there is not a standardized style of what the couple is prepared to comment on; because everybody is different and in their view of what their union is going to be. Traditionally the couple's hands are tied together; but in this case, it does not have to be, the chosen element of service.
Again an outdoor ceremony can be perfect, to reenact going around the fire pit three times; they leap over the fire, the water dish and the broom right next to it on the ground.
Where unconditional love, is divinely dedicated and with a great awareness not to misrepresent, the "perfect love and perfect trust" commitments, of such said conditions. From the union of all creation and as the water is to the chalice, the couple can drink. There are a lot of different meanings, for the couple to play around with and make appropriate; as in the case with the phallic interpretation of the knife and goblet as the womb.

The Family Celebrant & Officiant

MODIFICATION And ADAPTATION:

The wine can be placed on the focal counter and/or a round table; because not everyone believes in altars. Perfect for when the ceremony, can be performed outdoors and with a fire, that the gathering aspires around. A hand ceremony can be made very appropriate here and with the right script to accompany a reading for it. A coin can also be placed, into the couples hands and as it would have originally, during their nuptials.

This unity ritual also has its claims from the Hispanic culture and is known, as the "LASSO AND COIN CEREMONY".

The Lasso is a cord that represents their infinite bond and like a figure eight, it is placed around their shoulders; after the exchange of vows. The coin exchange can also be incorporated with the ring exchange or made separately and to replace the ring exchange. The coin exchange is to break the stereo type bread winner and home maker; to signify equality in the give and take relationship. This relationship that has outgrown the two and to accept the mutual support of children and the stewardship for all couples alike. To finalize with the Wiccan concept and original betrothal; a piece of charcoal too, would have been collected and/or from their first fire together. The wine is then placed on the altar. A loaf of bread is then taken and torn open above their heads; "so they may never know hunger". The Celebrant can say " MAY YOU NEVER KNOW HUNGER". Then "WITH THIS COIN THAT HAS BEEN GIVEN ONCE AGAIN MAY YOU NEVER KNOW WANT " ("Never be without"). By this time the old coal has been given back to the fire; a new one from this point of reference, is placed into their hands. "MAY YOUR HEARTS NEVER BE COLD AND ALWAYS HAVE FIRE ". The couple, then takes the bread and wine; around the circle to share it with everyone there.

Knowing what we have learned from the above partial and completed versions of Wicca; why not take and modify?

Chapter Five ~ Renewal of Vows ceremony

A "SAND CEREMONY(usually placed after the ring exchange) would be perfect in this case. Where the old rings can be placed in and then the new ones can be held. Warming of the rings Passing of the rings. spend a few seconds giving their blessing and well wishes, before passing the rings on to the next person. With some nice music playing in the background and the time will lapse smoothly. Sand is a perfect conductor for consecrating; the clearing of old energies and from it, an appropriate blessing for the old rings, so that they can be warn again.

The sand ritual element, can also involve the family; each member having their own colour of sand.

Dollar stores, can carry, a wide variety of sand colours.

With the "Coin Exchange": the couple exchanges the coins and as they repeat, a certain pledge; to take care of the kids, and/or not to any more; because they are living on their own and it is just the two of them. To make a pledge and dedicate a new provision, of care for each other and their home.

Then a sand poring ritual can take place. Where the Celebrant announces to the couple by name; and pledges to each other that in "closing here today". "This relationship will be made symbolic through the pouring of each individual containers of sand into the one that firstly the couple will pour into and that of their old rings; then each and every other member of the family to combine into this one glass. "One, representing you, Bethany and the other representing you Janine and all that you were, all that you are, and all that you will ever be". "Please Blend the Sand". "As these two containers of sand are poured into the third container, the individual containers of sand will no longer exist, but will be joined together as one". "Just as these grains of sand can never be separated, our prayer for you today is that ……".

The Sand Ceremony perhaps, originated from, when a couple came from a different birth place(to take the sand and pour it into one) than the other.

The Family Celebrant & Officiant

MODIFICATION And ADAPTATION:

A Hand Lei Ceremony, is also similar to a hand fastening; however this is where one coin and charcoal can be placed in their hands. It is a practice of the Hawaiian natives and can incorporate this blessing with the Wiccan traditional coin and piece of charcoal. The couple is asked to face each other; rather than a lei to be placed over and around their hands, they just hold hands. Then the Hawaiian blessing, is recited and/or modified and as with the previous, betrothal chapter two(A Gay Ceremony Commitment Rough drafting Script); It will start with,
"THESE ARE THE HANDS".

A Unity Candle Lighting ritual,

is always a good addition for this, very simple and most elegant Renewal Of Vows Ceremony; where the partners, could light from their own personal candle and/or, sample the following:
Celebrant: "To remind us of these two lives united once again, we ask Lawrence and Jeanine's children to come forward".
"Have you any words for this couple?
Celebrant: "Lawrence, this candle represents you.
We ask your children to light your flame; as your spark before provided for their own existence years ago".
[Children light candle] **Celebrant**: "Jeanine, this candle represents you. We ask your children to light your flame; as your spark before provided for their own existence years ago".
[Children light candle] **Celebrant**: "Jeanine and Lawrence, this candle represents your new found union and renewed from this day forward. Can you both accept this new chapter of your lives and with the remaining passion of your own ?
"We ask that you light this flame of joy together and with each other".
Whether be it, a silver 25th year and/or a 50th gold anniversary. Ultimately, why not create your very own and un-thought of rituals, to add into your services?

Ceremony Guide   CSOC

Chapter Five ~ Renewal of Vows ceremony

In order to add value to this type of ceremony; a very explicit package is provided and in the following business module.

" BESPOKE YOUR CEREMONY "

Renewing your wedding vows? Congratulations! There are a variety of reasons, for a wide variety of words that can be expressed "to do this " and over again" .

Renewing Your Wedding Vows for an Anniversary ~ to re-pledge after 25 yrs the love and commitment or even 50yrs. As husband and wife, the presence of God and all that make up the community of friends and family alike. Pledge for another promise full of eternal love that will await the both of you to make again that life may bring.

Renewing Your Wedding Vows After an Infidelity, Illness or other Stressful Time

The past may have tested those vows, but your enduring love for one another has prevailed. Re-pledge the many things again to her, including your faithfulness.
With great sorrow and regret, that you will once again acknowledge that you broke that vow but now do realize, the enormity of this mistake and to reaffirm this love and commitment. Once again a fresh start, to renew these vows of love, honour, and fidelity from the other side of the mountain, and to continue life's journey by each other's side. Promise to love you, honour and get to keep her all over again better than before.

Vow Renewal After a Private Wedding or Small Wedding

Your family and friends first showed you how to love, helped you grow, and supported you when you found each other. With this ceremony they can continue to love and support you even more as you love and support them. Although witnesses are optional a second time around; maybe your children could be the ones to give you away this time and do the witnessing. Those who were around you in the past to witness might not be and as close to you as those who, in the presence of these witnesses, to reaffirm this commitment can be made available.

Getting a Church Blessing

Peerless Moments is a spiritual metaphysical methodology, creatively combined to accommodatingly accepts all faiths. Typically the words you will say at a vow renewal are the same words you would say at any type of wedding.

The Officiant may make remarks about renewal, and any songs or readings may speak specially of lasting love or rebirth.

Speak with your Officiant about what is appropriate in your religion.

The Family Celebrant & Officiant

" BESPOKE YOUR CEREMONY "

What Actually Happens During the Ceremony?

You'll exchange vows, recalling what you said when you were first married.
You could also vary the wordings and write a better vow this time around.
What a great opportunity for the both of you to really think about how you feel about your relationship. The of the exchange rings can be your original bands with new engravings (perhaps the date of your vow renewal or a meaningful quotation) or new rings purchased expressly for the reaffirmation(a great time to upgrade those bands, if you want to). Children, close relatives and special friends can do readings, and you can have meaningful music playing, just as you would at a wedding ceremony. When you think about how long it took to save up and/or even plan the first time around and/or that this time around you want to take the time to really make it meaningful. This second time around will not be as stressful because you both have become closer to each other and your community from the experience. The shyness will have cleared away and the roleplaying will excite the passion for each other to express upon and expand; while exploring the many opportunities at your avail much more freely than before.

~*Various Rituals*~

A traditional variety of customs can be included in a ceremony. Some old, some new, and some just imagined in the moment whils growing in popularity. Below are some examples:

Circling: The unbroken circle of commitment to each other can have a variety of ways to perform, such as they do in Eastern European customs; where you both circle the altar three times as taking the first steps together. It does not have to be three times, in Hindu practices, the couple circles seven times around a ceremonial fire, to seal their bond. Whatever is best suited for you and the words from the ceremony script to give it extra meaning.

Unity Candles: You each take a lit candle and simultaneously light a third larger one("Unity Candle"). You may then blow out your individual candles, or leave them lit, symbolizing that you have both not lost your individuality in this unity together. There are many variations that can come about from this ceremony, and including to give all of your guests a candle. When the first guest's candle is lit; then all the other guests take from the first and pass it around. Finally the flame will reach the you both and as you both will light the "Unity Candle" together. This variation typically includes a proclamation that this ceremony represents the unity of friends and family supporting the couple in their marriage.

Salt Ceremony: (Hindu weddings traditions), where one of you can pass a handful of pink Himalayan salt to the other and without spilling any; you then pass it back to the other and the exchange is repeated three times. Then each of you both can perform this salt exchange with all the members of the other's family, to symbolize your blending in with the other new family.

Ceremony Guide   CSOC

Chapter Five ~ Renewal of Vows ceremony

Peerless Moments

" BESPOKE YOUR CEREMONY "

~*Various Rituals*~

Musical performance: can be included prior to the ceremony for guests to enjoy; while they take their seats (prelude), while the groom/groomsmen (optional), bridesmaids and bride (procession) enter the ceremony, while certificate keepsake parchment(s) are being signed and/or any other activity that requires it (interlude) and afterwards the ceremony, in closing (recession).

Wine Ceremony: You each take a nice glass pitcher(carafe)and pour some into a
single glass, where you will both drink from.

The **Quaich: Pronounced as "Quake", it is a two handled cup type variation; to represent the trust and unity between you both. It can be filled with your favourite champagne/wine and/or water, either before or during the ceremony. At the appropriate moment, one of you will pick it up by the handles, and then the other partner will place hands on the other's and as you take turns drinking together.

Water Ceremony: Where you as a couple will each pour a different coloured water into a single glass
and thus creating a third colour together.

Garland/Lei Ceremony: Common amongst Hindu tradition and similar to the Hawaiian.
You both exchange Your neck-laced flower pieces with one another, as a token of love and respect; that you have for each other in these "Leis". You can also include many other of these floral neck-laced pieces, to unite and bring the family closer; as well as, friends and others of such likeness to participate.

Sand Ceremony: Similar to the water ceremony, you both pour different coloured sand into a glass, taking turns, and just a little at a time to create clourful patterns and swirls. After the ceremony and festivities conclude, jar is typically sealed by pouring hot wax into the top of the jar, and then capping it with a cork stopper or other such lid. This can help to preserve the swirls and make a nice display item for the home. Other variations can include: the children or other family members of yours, each having a different coloured sand and taking turns to pour.
Another variation can include for each side of the family to fill with one glass with different coloured sands, and then the other side of the family to fill a second glass. Then the both of you will take from your side of respective mixes to alternately fill another larger container mixing the two into this larger one.
NOTE*: Coloured sands, carafes and vases can be found at many crafts stores.

Breaking Bread Ceremony: In that, "you may never know of hunger"; you as the couple, tear off a piece of bread to eat. The bread can then be passed around to share with family and friends.

© 2019 Canadian Society of Celebrants

The Family Celebrant & Officiant

Peerless Moments

" BESPOKE YOUR CEREMONY "

Handfastings, **Commitment Ceremonies**; **Renewals** and **Baby Naming**

CEREMONY PACKAGES:

Starting Fee

Renew Your Wedding Vows for an Anniversary ?
After an Infidelity, Illness or other Stressful Time ?
After an Elopement or a Small Private Nuptial?

Renewal of Vows Ceremony

This could be a small gathering at someone's home or a large party in a reception hall.

From --- $ 359

- **Consultation** of Ceremony package
  Interview(Anatomy of Ceremony)
- **Unlimited telephone meetings and online consultations**
- **A short rehearsal**
- **Renewal of Vows, signed proof of keepsake certificate**
  (optional) A keepsake copy of Ceremony script
- **Adding elements**(ex. a sand ceremony) **can make for a nice touch too!**
- **Up to 30 minutes Ceremony duration & Exquisite Script Design:** Poetry/readings, photos, videos, music, audience sing along and guest participation rites, etc., can also be tastefully added, to a ceremony and for that personal touch.

. **TRAVEL EXPENSES ~**
Anything over a 30km range is subject to an additional $2/km consideration.

- NB: 50% Initial Deposit Fee is Payable before starting and with a 25% Non- Refundable.
- Final Agreed Invoice to be paid in full on the day of Ceremony and before the paperwork signing.

© 2019 Canadian Society of Celebrants   4

Ceremony Guide   CSOC

Chapter Five ~ Renewal of Vows ceremony

Peerless Moments

" BESPOKE YOUR CEREMONY "

Special Ceremony Elements

- **NOTE*** With some exceptions to pricing:
  ALL OTHER ELEMENTS FROM THE ACTUAL PURCHASE OF PRODUCT WILL HAVE A **25% MARK-UP** FROM THEIR RETAIL PRICE + TAXES INCLUDED; AND FURTHER ENHANCEMENTS TO DESIGN WILL BE FURTHER NEGOTIABLE WITH ALL SAID PARTIES PRIOR TO.

Signing & Witness Ceremony

- **Renewal of Vows, signed proof of keepsake certificate**
  --**from $50**(no glass frame)

- A brief ceremony involving the couple and 2-4 witnesses; each in turn sign the keepsake parchment.

Unity Sand Ceremony Option

- Originally designed as a sand clock; that can symbolically refresh your union every time you turn it over. Just like each grain to value the importance of each moment together. A great ritual option to involve the children in the joining of you as a couple.

Wine Box / Love Letter reveal

- To rewrite love letters to each other before the ceremony then seal in an envelope. During this anniversary celebration and to be added to the ceremony, to read out loud while sharing the wine(You can with the same bottle of wine or to replace it with another). When the day should come to part of ways, there will be something to remember through a loss and/or separation; whilst drinking the wine and reading the letters(why the falling in love and choice to be together happened in the first place).

Breaking of the Glass Ceremony

- The Breaking of the Glass Ceremony option to signify the end of the ceremony and the time of celebration. As a health & safety concern, the glass (often two champagne flutes) is placed in a cloth bag prior to breaking it.

© 2019 Canadian Society of Celebrants   5

The Family Celebrant & Officiant

Peerless Moments

" *BESPOKE YOUR CEREMONY* "

Special Ceremony Elements

American Indian Wedding Vase Ceremony
- This vase features two openings(drinking spouts) connected by a single handle and symbolizes with your vows, a renewing of your union.
- To drink simultaneously without spilling a drop, will bring you an intuitive understanding and with your renewed union together.

- CD/USB recorded music for the ceremony ----------------from $15 -$25 depending on the device and/or length and quality.
-

Smashing Coconuts
- A mentally stimulating and modified ritual, in connection with the Hindu God Ganesh; with sweet grass and boiled white rice. The coconuts are smashed, then the children pick the largest lucky pieces; to fill with a handful of rice, outside the entrance of the home, and every other entrance(south east corner of the home). It clears the static energy and obstacles they might encounter on their path and in their home together.

Warming of the rings
- Passing of the rings. spend a few seconds giving their blessing and well wishes, before passing the rings on to the next person.
- With some nice music playing in the background and the time will lapse smoothly.

- ### Group song/s at a wedding and/or a mass reading too
- No rehearsals required, no prior knowledge needed.
- The wording can also be included on your order of service.
- A simple print out of the words on to card or paper (one per pair) can be provided and be placed on the seats prior to the ceremony.

- ### Costs to be Agreed prior to Ceremony
- Travel expenses - $2per km if over 30 to venue / client.
- Accommodation – At Cost if overnight stay required.
- Fancy Dress – At Cost as required
- Miscellaneous Costs – As agreed (Reception MC / Toastmaster)

© 2019 Canadian Society of Celebrants

Ceremony Guide   CSOC

Chapter Five ~ Renewal of Vows ceremony

" *BESPOKE YOUR CEREMONY* "

Reminiscing on how to hold your ceremony? When thinking about the escort's origin: the right hand was always made available to draw a sword in the defending of the maiden's honour. Also, a bit of role playing, never hurt anyone and can be wonderfully selected, for a Shakespearian, English Script and Theme. The modern alternative, can also be implemented, for the Officiant, the gent, best gent, and groom(ette)s to enter from a side door, in a line, with the handmaidens and maiden of honour, proceeding down the aisle unescorted. Ring bearer was next, followed by the flower boy/girl (no one walked on the flower petals before the "Lady"), and finally the "Lady" and her son(or any other close family member), when choosing to be escorted. The "Lady" preferred to walk on the left side. In simple form, escorted by her lead, until she'd reach the front of the nave, and the escort would sit. Another popular tradition can have the Officiant ask "Who gives this "Lady" to this gent ?" Whilst she stands beside the Officiant awaiting; and perhaps one of your children and/or grandchildren can now respond "I do," or "your daughter/son and I do." (Or other appropriate answer). Then the "Lady" steps forward as the escort takes their seat. The groom(ette) also steps forward, to meet her in the middle.

What about the **"Hand Off"**? After answering the question, the escort can shake the hand of the gent, kiss the "Lady" on the cheek, and hand her over. In the simplest form, the escort, with their right hand, can take the "Lady's" *right* hand, from their left arm and place it in the gent's *left* hand. (Reminder tip:"Right, Right, Left, Left"). The gent takes a step forward during the transition and accepts the hand off.
* After the hand off, the "Lady" passes her bouquet to the maid of honour, and faces the groom(ette), to place her left hand in her/his right *OR* just passes the bouquet, to face the Officiant, and turning later in the ceremony to face each other. Ceremony begins.

Note: It is not required for either the "Lady" to be escorted, nor to be "given away".

These traditions, are only to be considered and modified accordingly(as noted above).
A more modern variation of the processional, can use two aisles, with maidens entering from the left and their male role players, from the right. Typically in this option the "Lady" is not escorted. Instead, both parties walk and last in the procession down their aisle independently. The Officiant awaits for their arrival at the front. Ideally, mocking a "V" formation and from the back, coming together at the altar. Again improvising this from your space of venue and when two back corner doors are not available. Perhaps the arrangement of chairs, can better to accommodate the creation of two aisles. We must always work best with what we have; rather than expect and have unforeseen disappointments. Also there is no requirement to pose the question, of "who gives this woman"; you already have been there and have done that before; instead make it a common resonating question, such as: "In the presence of this gathering here today, do you both, accept each other anew, in marriage"? Knowing this much now culturally and about the standard, traditional patterns, of processionals; Why not modify the sequence and/or design an entirely different approach that can to best accommodate your circumstances and personalities?

© 2019 Canadian Society of Celebrants   8

The Family Celebrant & Officiant

" BESPOKE YOUR CEREMONY "

Since this is not a regular wedding service, you have several options.
You could both walk down the aisle with your children in tow, or the wife could walk to her husband alone, putting all the attention on her. You can exchange new rings; or give each other your old rings and to symbolize a renewed faith, in your marriage. Family members may do some readings in your honour. Many people don't think anyone should walk down the aisle alone; walking in with your partner and/or children, can add a special touch to the ceremony. You can also use this as an excuse to update your wedding bands. Maybe you've wanted to get new ones, or nicer ones for a long time, and this can be the perfect occasion.

Throw your old ones in a sand ritual glass and then seal the glass over with wax. Or opt to have the rings engraved with something special and to mark for this day. Although witnesses are not important, a certificated that can be witnessed can make for a great keepsake.

Celebrate at your reception: Peerless Moments can offer to help with the occasion and by providing the scripted toast Master intro; that can spark participants from the gathering and an invite to add lib theirs. This could be a small gathering at someone's home or a large party in a reception hall. You have many options here as well. Have a first dance between you and your spouse to your favourite song and don't make a big deal out of the father-daughter dance. Rather than the elaborate cake cutting ritual; why not have a potluck and/or serve cupcakes instead? You can ask people to prepare ahead of time their toasts and with your very own.

In honour of your lasting love, and even a new house warming; Peerless Moments can come up with a memorable script in the helpful gathering of information such as this. We can help to prompt the public speaking and without us even having to be there, to Officiate. As a matter of fact, why not ask Peerless Moments, to be the master of ceremonies or toastmaster at the reception ? You can also bring your original wedding album or have photos of your original wedding available so that your guests can reminisce about your wedding. You might even have some photographs that commemorated the event handy for this event.

There are many variations on how your wedding renewal ceremony and reception should be done. Perhaps the ceremony can make room and give some space within the script that we can help design with you; to give toasts to the important guests. By those you choose to focus on and express how much they have meant to you over the years; might be stirred enough to give a toast and many others too, many times in return!

Write your vows. The "Renewal Of Vows" ceremony, agenda is intended on your continued love for your spouse; the focal point revolves around a niche, the writing of your own vows. Peerless Moments, can write something, to say and in addition to the traditional ceremony readings. You also don't have to write your own. You can have the Officiant say whatever you want on your behalf, and to reaffirm your love that way. We can ask questions like, "will you continue to have so and so, as your wife and to continue your happy and loving marriage?" To reaffirm your commitment to one another, all you have to do, is answer back, "I will,".

Ceremony Guide CSOC

Chapter Five ~ Renewal of Vows ceremony

Peerless Moments

" BESPOKE YOUR CEREMONY "

- *Ceremony- Interview Checklist*

CONTACT DETAILS
Client 1 (Preferred Name)
Client 2 (Preferred Name)
Address
Email_____ 2nd Email:_____ .
Phone #'s
CEREMONY FOR: Full Name Bride / Groom Occupation: DOB: Where?: Full Name Bride / Groom Occupation: DOB: Where?:
Intended Salutation : Mr & Mrs / Mr & Mr /Mrs & Mrs ? **Married Name :**

© 2019 Canadian Society of Celebrants

The Family Celebrant & Officiant

" BESPOKE YOUR CEREMONY "

Ceremony- Interview Checklist

PARTICIPATING FRIENDS & RELATIVES:	Client 1	Client 2
Brothers		
Sisters		
Children		
Pets		
Friends		
Witnesses / Others		
Theme?:		
Ceremony Officiant Dress(will cost extra if not provided for the certain costume theme) ?:		
Agreed Extras: Costume Hire Travel Accommodation		
Do you want to include witnesses ?	YES / NO Renewal of Vows, signed proof of keepsake certificate(optional) YES / NO (please circle)	

© 2019 Canadian Society of Celebrants   11

Ceremony Guide   CSOC

Chapter Five ~ Renewal of Vows ceremony

Peerless Moments

" BESPOKE YOUR CEREMONY "

Ceremony- Interview Checklist

Location?: **Accessibility?:** **Contingency?:**	
Special Elements: Handfasting Unity Ceremony Broom Jumping Rose Ceremony Parchment Ring Warming	
Reception?: Is it to be included with Ceremony Script Where & When? *NOTE A separate Script For RECEPTION and on its Own, will have additional costs to it. *(ex. House Warming Party)* MC /TOASTMASTER Will Toasts be included in the Ceremony Script Please add details from ? And WHOM the Participants the information is coming from. Anything Else?	

© 2019 Canadian Society of Celebrants   12

The Family Celebrant & Officiant

" BESPOKE YOUR CEREMONY "

About your relationship?

Think about how you felt when you first met, what made you fall in love and when you knew you wanted to spend the rest of your lives together. Write it all out to get your creative gears turning.

> A fully customized ceremony will require for the
> Officiant to design a ceremony that reflects your love story.
> A truly a unique ceremony for each couple, and all about you.
> It can be religious or non-religious, you decide!
> Make your ceremony exactly what you want, and not the stuffy boring Ceremony that everyone has seen in the past.
> Be as open as possible and do not worry because anything potentially hurtful and/or embarrassing will not be publicly shared and/or during your ceremony!
> Remember, the more information you provide, the more meaningful picture of who you are can become more colourful.
> Feel free to add additional Q&A lines if needed, if you have something you really want to share that is not listed.

Personalized Vows

Can be written by either or both partners and ==at an extra cost==; you can even ask us, ==to simply write it for you==. Personalized vows can help you express your love for one another and promise to support and love each other for many years to come.
No matter what you choose - be it traditional, religious or personalized vows - remember the focus of your wedding should be on you.

The Wedding Vows / ==What do you prefer==?

Your vows may run from traditional to customize. Feel free to add your own embellishments, loving words, funny promises(I promise to take the trash out!) and inside jokes. Also, couples may like pieces of several of the vow examples, while not finding any one example that completely reflects their preferences. ==Pieces from several can be blended together to make the "perfect" one.== (Please specify by circling 1of 3)

There are 3 formats or "styles" ==for vows (and also ring exchanges==):==Please specify for both==

1. **Echo** - Officiant says "Please repeat after me", then reads the vow one line at a time, with participant repeating each line, one line at a time, until the vow is complete.

2. **I Do** - Officiant begins with "Do you", then reads the entire vow, followed by the participant's response of "I do"

3. **Recital** - a more personal vow, spoken from memory while looking directly into the partner's eyes, and without prompt by officiant. This format can be tricky, especially if the vows are long and complex.

Ceremony Guide   CSOC

Chapter Five ~ Renewal of Vows ceremony

Peerless Moments

" BESPOKE YOUR CEREMONY "

Here's a handy list of questions to help get you started:

Why did you decide to renew your vows in the first place?	
What hard times have you gone through together?	
What have you supported each other through?	
What are you most looking forward to about your life together, after this event?	
What do you want to accomplish more together?	
What makes your relationship tick?	
Can you remember when you first met and has anything changed since?	
When did you realize you were in love? When did you first say, "I love you?"	
What do you most respect about your partner?	
How has your life gotten better since meeting your mate?	
What about them inspires you?	

© 2019 Canadian Society of Celebrants   14

The Family Celebrant & Officiant

" BESPOKE YOUR CEREMONY "

list of questions to help get you started:

When was your first date and what was it like?	
Where & How did you meet?	
When did you "know" that they were the right person?	
What do you see when you think about your longer-term future together?	
Can you remember how you proposed to one another Who did the proposing; How is this any different from then?	
How did you get married before?	
What are your nicknames for each other? Have they changed?	
What's something quirky or unique about your relationship?	
What do you like to do together? (keep it rated PG)	

ANYTHING ELSE ? Feel free to add other pertinent information

Ceremony Guide   CSOC

Chapter Five ~ Renewal of Vows ceremony

" BESPOKE YOUR CEREMONY "

YOUR Vows

Finally, will you share them with each other or keep them a secret until the *ceremony* day?

Will you write them separately : Yes/No
Please circle and let the officiant know
or together: Yes/No

This is meant to be helpful to us and not to make you feel at all uncomfortable.
Your answers will be very helpful in preparing this ceremony.
Remember, to send them only back to us and let us know
We will save a copy of your answers in your file.
Decide how you want your vows to come across, agree on the format and tone with each other.
One tip: "Include promises that are broad in scope, such as 'I promise to always support you,' as well as very specific to the two of you, like 'I promise to say "I love you" every night before bed,'"

Do you envision them as humorous?

Poetic and romantic?

Will they be completely different or will you make the same promises to each other as you would with traditional vows(you can do a little of each)?

We know some of the questions are intense and you do not have answer all of them.

3. Recital - a more personal vow, spoken from memory while looking directly into the partner's eyes, and without prompt by officiant. This format can be tricky, especially if the vows are long and complex. A written text (cheat sheet) tucked in a sleeve for backup is a good idea for this option. If yours are running longer than 3 minutes, makes some edits. Put some of the more personal thoughts in a letter or gift to your fiancé on the morning of your wedding and save any guest-related topics for your toasts.

The Family Celebrant & Officiant

<u>A House Warming Party</u>

There comes a time when the family, a couple has created; reaches a maturity level, of young adults. The couple too, has reached the next chapter of their lives, called "downsizing". Most of the time this special occasion, is perfectly held for a proposal, as well as for a Renewal of Vows.
The following example, has done just that.

Husband: Accustomed as I am to public speaking.
I am simply going to say, thank you very much
for coming and as I stand aside, to introduce my wife.

PAUSE-1-2-3-4-→

Wife: Never let it be said; that we do things the easy way. This downsizing has been one of the most challenging. You all know how we got together, and you all know why we moved away. We have come full circle once again, as newlyweds and when we first moved in together; in this town and as it was a smaller place. Very convenient and almost, just as expensive. Now with David and I, retired and the children, well you all know. Perhaps before we start the ceremony, to renew our vows; they might have a few things to say as well. Staying in that big old house, gave us a bit of an empty nest syndrome. It's been difficult for us; but it is good to be back home. With so many familiar faces and to see you all here, comfortably close and cozy; around the fire place, and Sun Valley View, retirement village. It is so wonderful to be with all you folk and right next to the Atlantic shore, watching the Sun set. All me and David want now, is for a quiet life together.

Husband nods and kisses her hand

PAUSE-1-2-3-4-→

Ceremony Guide   CSOC

Chapter Five ~ Renewal of Vows ceremony
A House Warming Party

Wife: Emily and Tom, our Son; would also, well I assume, be is here to wish us well?

Pause-*2-3-4-5*-- →

Tom(eldest son):YES- of course...I hope that you will be very happy here together. I am glad that you have forgiven us, your children; for thinking a nursing home was better fit than this and Gemma too, for inviting herself here. Ultimately and as I can speak on behalf of us all is that you can forgive us and everything that has happened and for us to simply move on past it. Well we all wish what's best and father gets to keep his Mercedes and his sail boat; so it must be a win-win for us all. I am hoping, you and father, have the peace and quiet; that you both deserve, from now on.

Pause-*2-3-4-5* → ==*Tom's marriage proposal, to his girlfriend(Emily)*.==

Wife(Jessica): With a long list of people to thank, it might be less annoying, to introduce to you, our Ceremony Officiant.

Pause-*2-3-4-5*-- → ==*Celebrant introduction ....AND....*==
Pause-*2-3-4-5* →

Celebrant: So brace yourselves now, here we go; with the Wine Box/Love Letter reveal. This time, however you will all become participants. Let us firstly reflect on all the good and warming thoughts; to bring into this house, of early memories and of how you have all came to know David and Jessica. Write your blessings, from the heart and of the many memories, down on your pieces of paper; whilst the wine box gets passed around.

Fold your paper, nicely and place it in the box.
==*SO YOU KIND OF GET A ROUGH IDEA THEN*==?

The Family Celebrant & Officiant

<u>The following sample, is of a completed client's script copy:</u>

" BESPOKE YOUR CEREMONY "

Sample of Client Copy

RENEWAL OF VOWS CELEBRATION

FOR

LAWRENCE(LARRY) SEWELL & JEANINE LAVAL

Tuesday, March 27th, 2018

5pm

Sewell Residence
500 Kingston Rd. Scarborough, Ontario, M4L 1V3

© 2018 Canadian Society of Celebrants

Ceremony Guide   CSOC

Chapter Five ~ Renewal of Vows ceremony

" *BESPOKE YOUR CEREMONY* "

WEDDING CEREMONY for LAWRENCE(LARRY) SEWELL & JEANINE LAVAL
At roughly 5pm the Celebrant will enter
background music must stop

• **Processional Music**
Music *Sysyphe - Handfasting(Magic Wedding)*

During this time; the ring warming ceremony will start off and finish, upon the bride/groom entrance. I will start by taking the rings(tied with red string Jeanine's and green Lawrence's and held together by the white string) together in my hands, for a moment of silence; to visualize a blessing or two for them.
I will then pass it along to the next person and that person will do the same, passing it along to the next; until all of us, who want to make a wish, or give a blessing for you Jeanine and Lawrence. The rings are passed along and finally(strings are cut/removed)end up again, in the hands of your best friend; who will then pass the ring to each of you, to place on around your finger, during the vows.

Processional
Entrance of the bride/groom; as you both come in a *synchronistic way* and from opposite sides, to join together. Upon entry, you must take shoes off and be greeted, by grand-daughter/son; with the basket of flower petals. They will follow the both of you down; casting a circular path of petals and from each side. You are to follow their lead, until they meet at the center and where a bunch of petals are already there for you to both stand on.

CELLEBRANT: Gives a little introduction.

Please stand to greet the bride You may be seated, thank you.

Good afternoon everybody. Welcome to the residence of the Sewell's and welcome to this "Renewal Of Vows Ceremony" For Jeanine and Lawrence. My name is . .   . .   , as your Celebrant I am honoured, to be called out and for this exciting occasion. Alternatively, please silence your phones. The ceremony is about to begin.

The Family Celebrant & Officiant

" BESPOKE YOUR CEREMONY "

Cellebrant:

In this gathering here today, we celebrate one of life's greatest moments, the rejoining of two hearts. Anyone present, who has just cause why this couple should not be reunited again and perhaps differently, in this way..... Sussh! I want to also bring to your attention, that this time around Larry's parents and Jeanine's father; that we can rather to welcome and acknowledge their spiritual presence. We feel their presence with us today, and take joy in this knowledge; that they would all be thrilled, to see this reunion come to life again, with bride, groom and the likes of all of you, as their admirers.

OPENING

Cellebrant:

Lawrence and Jeanine, today you are surrounded by your family and friends; all of whom are gathered, to witness your exchange of vows and to share in the joy, of this occasion. Your renewal of vows is a statement that from here and forward from this day; on what you will continually mean to each other and to the refreshed commitment, of this here marriage.

I would like to now bring forward your beloved Son Joseph Sewell to read out loud the following poem called

"In Praise Of Love" by R.m.A.

© 2018 Canadian Society of Celebrants

Ceremony Guide   CSOC

Chapter Five ~ Renewal of Vows ceremony

" BESPOKE YOUR CEREMONY "

R.m.A:

'In Praise Of Love, We cannot know praise for, in any other way:

The bliss that love can offer, when in Love

It is the something, that deserves in us, to learn to praise.

To praise ourselves, once in a while, for our accomplishments.

That is the courage, of love and from it, the compassion that grows.

By giving praise to love, we might to feel, the sharing of its care, in others.

To feel love and give praise, to those dear and near to us,

Our mother, father, children and most of all our spouse.

To recognize praise, we must be receptive, through the eyes of love.

In praise of Love we filter through

For any other kind of praise, is likely a deception.

As it is doomed when not through love.

To be in Love and feel its praise.

We feel compassion growing more each day

It is the best kind of blissfulness there is.

In Praise Of Love, we can surrender.

© 2018 Canadian Society of Celebrants   4

The Family Celebrant & Officiant

" BESPOKE YOUR CEREMONY "

Celebrant.

Thanks Joseph for his speaking.

ADDRESS

Celebrant. Love Story

These two have more fun together; than they ever thought possible, with another human being, and they're smart people.

Once you find somebody, who makes every single day of your life better; who makes every single day more enjoyable, by golly, you have to hold on to that person.

When you love someone, you do not love them all the time and in exactly the same way, from moment to moment. It is an impossibility and even a lie to pretend to; yet this is exactly, what most of us demand.

We have so little faith, in the ebb and flow of life; of love and of relationships. We leap at the flow, of the tide and resist, in the terror of the ebb; because we are afraid, it will never return.

We insist on permanency, on duration, on continuity; when the only continuity possible, in life as in love, is in growth, in fluidity and in freedom.

Ceremony Guide   CSOC

Chapter Five ~ Renewal of Vows ceremony

" BESPOKE YOUR CEREMONY "

Celebrant. Love Story

The only real security, is not in owning or possessing, not in demanding or expecting and not in hoping, even. Security in a relationship, lies neither in looking back to what was and in nostalgia; not forward, to what it might be and in dread or anticipation. It's living in the present relationship and accepting each other; for who they are and in each moment, here and now!

THE BLESSING OF THE RINGS AND RENEWAL OF VOWS

Now comes for the big moment whilst the rings have come back around full circle, and with it the renewal of their vows. I would also like to bring to your attention; that after 33 years of wearing the same wedding bands.

Lawrence had decided on this great idea; to give to Jeanine, his ring of 33 years and that he has been wearing. In exchange, and as they had them properly fitted; Jeanine has agreed to do the same, for hers. Not only will Jeanine be getting Larry's ring to wear; but also his name engraved, on the inside and with it, the date, of when he had first started to wearing it.

With that said, Jeanine too, has done the same for Larry Sewell; however she too has creatively imagined up and with her very own idea, to shorten her name. The inscription now readable enough; "Jea" and with the number "9".

The Family Celebrant & Officiant

" BESPOKE YOUR CEREMONY "

THE BLESSING OF THE RINGS AND RENEWAL OF VOWS

Celebrant.

I bless these rings, that JEANINE LAVAL and LAWRENCE SEWELL, who give them, and who wear them, may ever abide in thy peace. Living together in unity, love and happiness for the rest of their lives to come. Both Jeanine and Lawrence will now renew their vows to each other and whilst exchanging rings. Firstly Jeanine, I gather you might have something to say about the rings; so why not start with your vows?

Jeanine and Lawrence both holding each other's ring to place on each other as they give their "I DO's" (one knuckle at a time).

Chapter Five ~ Renewal of Vows ceremony

" BESPOKE YOUR CEREMONY "

- **Vows**

Jeanine's: 33 years ago today, we skipped the betrothal and went straight to the nuptials. For the very first time this ring was placed on my finger, it fit just right for a size 6; the ring I give to you, in exchange for yours today has been enhanced to a size 9. It has been stretched and remolded so not to cut the circle of our this our very special bond to each other. Even in those moments that we were spared from and apart, 33 years has impressed upon it energetically and all the memories we hold so near and dear. In the tender loving embrace of stability and security; that I Jeanine will always be inseparable in my thoughts, with yours telepathically connected. The time has come, that we can share and grow with our hobbies; building on new things, to co-create and to fully explore our dreams together. Lawrence, my lover of all ages and throughout time eternal; I make this pledge to you and to be by your side, always. I Jeanine will accept you as my equal and with your flaws complete; to spend the rest remaining days together, with you Larry my love. To have the level of maturity to accept; that otherwise we could not change, in each other; to be that much more special and significant. I stand before you as a completed being and independent with my flaws, presenting to you this ring.

The Family Celebrant & Officiant

" *BESPOKE YOUR CEREMONY* "

- **Vows**

Lawrence's: I was vulnerably captivated from the instant rush of fascination and love for you. Jeanine, you are my inspiration, I hope that I can continue to be yours and if I haven't done so already, I will from here on forward.

My heart can elevate now and without all that seriousness, of struggling to survive; with nothing left to lose, I promise to be that extra bit more light hearted, than before. To take it easy and relax with new ideas; by reflecting back on all our struggles together it has grown in me a lot of compassion.

We have been through it all together and we have not neglected, to encourage with our sense of humour. You are my best friend, a true companion and my greatest motivation to get out of bed each day. With the children all grown and now with their own; we can sit back and marvel, on all the things we have and procreated together. I pledge to you my loyalty and sincerity; that I Lawrence Sewell, will invest on our hobbies together and future building endevours, I will take further interest, in us both, creatively and financially.

Let this ring I give to you be the reminder of our renewed bond and thoughtful communications; that we can all witness here together and together you Jeanine and I Lawrence Sewell with our love, be it the driving force.

Ceremony Guide   CSOC

Chapter Five ~ Renewal of Vows ceremony

" BESPOKE YOUR CEREMONY "

Celebrant.

Lawrence Sewell, can you please raise the hand, that you prefer the ring on.

Jeanine can you place the ring on and over the first knuckle of Lawrence's finger and hold it there, please.

Lawrence do you promise always to recognize Jeanine, as an equal individual and always to be conscious of her development, as well as your own.

With certainty, through kindness and faith, the life you have envisioned together as achievable; do you promise always to recognize Jeanine, as an equal individual; After hearing her vows to you, and that she has shared for us to witness, do you accept ?

Lawrence's Answer

Celebrant.

Jeanine, you may now push the ring down and above the other knuckle.

Lawrence Sewell, do you accept Jeanine again as spouse, in equal love, as a mirror for your true self, as a partner on your path, in tenderness and affection and in all the varying circumstances, of your lives together?

Lawrence's Answer

Jeanine, you may now push the ring completely down.

The Family Celebrant & Officiant

" BESPOKE YOUR CEREMONY "

Celebrant.

Jeanine Laval can you please raise the hand that you prefer to wear the ring on.

Lawrence can you place the ring and over the first knuckle of Jeanine's finger and hold it there, please.

Jeanine do you promise always to recognize Lawrence, as an equal individual and always to be conscious of his development, as well as your own.

With certainty, through kindness and faith, the life you have envisioned together as achievable; do you promise always to recognize Lawrence, as an equal individual; After hearing his vows to you, and that he has shared for us to witness, do you accept ?

Jeanine's Answer

Celebrant.

Lawrence, you may now push the ring down and above the other knuckle.

Jeanine Laval, do you accept Lawrence again as spouse, in equal love, as a mirror for your true self, as a partner on your path, in tenderness and affection and in all the varying circumstances, of your lives together?

Jeanine's Answer

Lawrence, you may now push the ring completely down.

© 2018 Canadian Society of Celebrants   11

Chapter Five ~ Renewal of Vows ceremony

" BESPOKE YOUR CEREMONY "

Celebrant.

To feel like gypsies felt, footloose and fancy free together, in their entrance into a new life and co-creative self expressions.

To symbolically "sweep away" their former enslaved lives, for newer adventures, as wife and husband. After they have jumped this broom, that lies before us on the floor, my announcement and their kiss will end our ceremony.

Jeanine/Lawrence, both hold each other's ring hand and Jump the Broom

Celebrant.

JEANINE & LAWRENCE your vows have rekindled your commitment to each other. The rings you are now wearing, is the symbol that you both have reunited as husband and wife again.

You may now kiss.

It has been my honour to officiate your ceremony today.

_____Thank you

- Parchment Signing with Music
- Recessional Music

The Family Celebrant & Officiant

PEERLESS MOMENTS SALES RECEIPT
BESPOKE YOUR CEREMONY

celebrant@msn.com
Toronto
416-920-5464
csoc@peerlessmoments.com

RECEIPT NO. 003
DATE March 7, 2018
CUSTOMER ID PM003

Larry L. Sewell
500 Kingston Rd.
Toronto ON. M4L 1V3
lsewell55@yahoo.com
416 694-8848

PAYMENT METHOD	Bank/e-transfers	Credit Card

QTY	Package #	DESCRIPTION	FULL AMOUNT	AMOUNT PAID
1.00	(standard	upto30min.RenewalOf	$ 359.00	$ 89.75

SUBTOTAL $ 89.75
TOTAL $ 359.00
OWING $ 269.25

Please pay the remaining balance in full by the day of Service !
THANK YOU FOR YOUR BUSINESS!

Ceremony Guide   CSOC

<u>Chapter Five</u> ~ Renewal of Vows ceremony

Certificate of Vow Renewal

This is to certify that

Jeanine and Lawrence Sewell

In celebration of thirty-three years of marriage

Renewed their wedding vows

on this Tuesday, Dated March 27ᵗʰ 2018

At_____

witnessed by:_____

this Ceremony

Signed:_____

Rev/Celebrant, Officiated this Ceremony.

The Family Celebrant & Officiant

Whether exchanging vows during a hand-fastening; whilst hands still bound and/or as simple, as lighting a candle.
The "Renewal of Vows" ceremony, is a rebirth of a couples commitment; a renaissance partnership, worth every moment in celebration. Expressing publically of their experiences, with each other and what is worth striving for. The strength to expose our vulnerable side and by accepting to forgive each other's flaws. A disclosure of new promises and reaffirm the old ones of compassion and integrity. To continue to cherish each other's uniqueness and restore the faith and belief in each other.
Perhaps, the only thing truer than one's first love, is to recommit to that love, before family and friends. In declaration of this love for life; from the heart that has loved, for so many given years and will continue to love, for as many more allots to it.

Treat yourselves and each other with respect;
be reminded often of what brought you together.
Give the highest priority to the tenderness,
gentleness and kindness; that your connection deserves.
When frustration, difficulties and fear assail your relationship,
as they threaten all relationships, at one time or another,
remember to focus on what is right between you,
not only the part which seems wrong.
In this way, you can ride out the storms and
when clouds hide the face of the sun in your lives...
Remember that in every given moment, the sun is still there;
when your faith has dwindled.
You both must take responsibility for the quality of your life together; then it will be marked by abundance and delight.
For where two or three are gathered together collectively and believing in a higher power, there it will be in the midst of them.
A modified take away, from the religious version of
Matthew's blessing for a marriage, by the Corinthians 18:20

Chapter Six ~ This is It

To recap: During the Initial Meeting/ The Interview Checklist:

When dealing with a couple's ceremony, Questions like:
"*I need to get to know you better as a* couple"; Or "*How would you describe your relationship*"? It is a little insight, as to who they are, as people. Why not, also ask the family; what they really like about them, individually and as a couple. These sort of questions can really get the family talking; in particular, look out for recollections that bring a smile or a laugh. Or get the couple to pretend, to imagine meeting their beloved for the first time? What they would think of them right now; versus, how they thought of them the first time, that they met, and get them to describe each other. The essential information needed, is mainly gained in an unhurried interview with the family.
Rather than the couple remembering their love story, why not get the best man and even maid of honour involved; to share a few stories of their own? It can make for a great addition, for after, during the reception and when giving a toast.
Have your clients requested a non religious ceremony?
Then ask them; on what, the kind of reading material and preference might be. The Celebrant (or designated person) must then go about the creative writing and carefully selecting the most appropriate quotes of poetry and literature. Every detail of the Ceremony Draft, must be carefully rechecked with the family and to ensure that, it is accurate. It can be very practical, to check with your clients song preferences and/or, the venue's musical selections ahead of time.

The Family Celebrant & Officiant

What happens after the initial meeting?

Approving the Ceremony & Transcript Delivery:

Often, the Ceremony Transcript previously prepared requires to be modifying. Always inform your clients of the many options; because they might want to review the Ceremony transcript prior to the Ceremony. Does it flow well with their event's Order of Service and to adapt with your Anatomy of the Ceremony Script?

Modification of the Ceremony Script:

Tweaking the script can be necessary, in all circumstances and for approval, prior to the Ceremony. Arranging for an online follow-up connection, might be the only way, things can be done; since "Covid-19", that could very well be the case.

What Questions Should You Ask? As mentioned earlier, while it is important to be flexible and to allow an interview to "digress", is where the "Interview Checklist" can be helpful. When having difficulties with pronunciation; write the place name phonetically, in your copy of the Ceremony script.

Ceremony particulars have been given in the sample templates (in the previous pages). When you feel you need more input, then go back over your notes and start the conversation again; by referring to something previously mentioned. Ask them to elaborate on something particular and that might script worthy; make certain, it is mentioned, in the right context.

Ultimately, with compassion, sincerity and great care, the Celebrant and/or with accompanying mentor, will be ready to Officiate the Ceremony. These tools that have been given, are proven methods; designed to help you along the way.

Now the time is ripe for the Final Draft; you can do this, so how about it? Produce your own ceremony menu, for the provision of and any other occasion, that you feel are worthy for a celebration.

Chapter Six ~ This is It

During the Ceremony and After

- **Always make yourselves, available for photographs**.

  Ask the client ahead of time for permission to advertise and request they send you the photographs and/or live videos social media links/threads. You might not want to place extra pressure and for written permission before hand; by asking the client for copies, of any photos that include them and you. Chances are, you might never get to see them otherwise? The family might even require, that you remain to be included in their photographs, before and/or after; just be guided by whoever, is the assigned photographer and/or filming company. Make an effort to be present after the show; whether you have been included, or not and stick around until the photographs have been taken. Chances are, you might never get to see these clients again; or the photos, they have agreed at that time. You could offer to pay the photographer, or filming company and with your client's permission; to use those links/photographs/video, in your publicity material?

- **Reception** – Some clients will invite you to their reception, most will not; as a professional and what you do with your career, is your decision. Unless you have prepared a separate script for the occasion and/or, are the public speaker or Officiant/M.C.; it is not highly recommended.
  Not unless, you are personally related and or involved; otherwise, it would be considered unprofessional, to be there. You might be sending the obvious message of freeloading and if that wasn't enough? Do not be fooled into thinking, that you could get more business this way; that is not the ideal place, for passing around your business cards.

The Family Celebrant & Officiant

During the Ceremony and After

- **Follow ups** – Take stock, to check up on your clients once in a while. Whether it be through social media platforms or from your own platform, as a social influencer and/or send them an email to get some feedback. Don't be shy, to contact them the old fashion way either, by phone to talk to them, to exchange pleasantries and ask for feedback; or a follow up thank you card/letter via airmail post. Reviews can be wonderful, perhaps direct them with links and where they can find the sites directly(website, email, blog, social media); can have a profound positive effect on generating new business. Chances are your clients have already passed around your business cards and also have recommend you to others. Word of mouth, is the best advertising gossip there is and amongst all demographics; it will never go out of style and will always be, the best utilized, local marketing tool.

There are many reasons that we share in life's celebrations with those we love. Ritual itself is designed to cause a change in our lives. The promises that a couple makes must be practical promises that when lived by will actually help them to safeguard their future. Another important aspect of ritual is that in being here we somehow feel closer to the couple by being allowed a peek into their inner most thoughts and feelings at this intensely personal moment of their lives. It reminds the couples here of when it was their special day and the promises they once made, and allows us all to somehow feel closer to one another as the community of family and friends that we truly are.
As Canadian Society Of Celebrants, we must be open to provide a safe, culturally appropriate, inclusive service for all people, regardless of their ethnicity, faith, ability, sexuality, or gender identity.

Chapter Six ~ This is It
What else is there ?
We could care to add the "==COMING OF AGE And COMING OUT CEREMONY==" to this list. These type of initiations, have played a vital role in all cultures throughout history.

Modern society has acceptable in this way of celebration to have become more important than ever before. The coming of age and gender acceptance; just the same, for who they are and have become. As early as the age of 13, sweet 16, and/or a marking of a major achievement in their adolescent life.

It can provide the strength in numbers and community support; to oversee them with given permission and encouragement to graduate and walk hand in hand, with their LGBTQ partners, when prom night rolls around. We all go through identity crisis, experience all kinds of transitions and in all stages of our life; however adolescence, has to be hormonally the greatest of impact and oftentimes, it creates psychological distress.

These ceremonies can encourage the young person's emotional well-being; the boost within society and most inner circles.

We can help provide with ceremony, the guidance; for the attention that these youth deserve into adulthood. As adults we can help provide the safe environment; to share our experiences and wisdom, from one generation to the next. As we are there to help guide along; we must also, from a level of maturity, allow and for the designing of a meaningful ceremony, to come from the child's input. At whatever stage of life; youth, middle age, crisis and/or retirement; all events must be considered and be made tribute to. Through ceremony these experiences can be celebrated; to actively be embraced as initiations, rather than denied, as emotional traumas. Creating ceremonies, that revolve around intense growth or dramatic, hormonal and psychological changes, is an art form; It mustn't be entirely dismissed and/or neither overlooked, for its healing properties.

The Family Celebrant & Officiant

What else is there ?

Celebrating authenticity might help to empower and overcome from the minority classifications; that otherwise would have us as marginalized, why not celebrate our differences instead?
To embody wisdom and maturity, does not have to be exclusive; whilst hurling the others, from such dignity and reverence, into a midlife crisis. Rather it must become inclusive, to suggest, that is acceptable LGBTQ for all. "What are we grateful for"?

- Whether it be retirement/valuing employees and/or layoffs/promotions; downsizing and adjusting to corporate merging/promotions; launching a new business, with your products and/or services; opening a new office; going into a partnership. Groupings of civil and corporate, as well as private business enterprises; they are all, just as entitled, to a ceremony. Make yourselves available and to help create, meaningful scripted ceremonies; for all social environment, levels and caste systems.

Throwing a party, is just another way of expressing gratitude; regardless the theme, of the celebration and the tone of the ceremony; mostly always, it revolves around "GRATITUDE". What is it that we appreciate and value most?

What are we most genuinely interested to consider and in the caring of others; rather than the feeling of fearful concern, to help leverage our misinterpretations for compassion?

Chapter Six ~ This is It
What else is there ?

HOW ABOUT A HOUSEWARMING CELEBRATION?

Throwing a party of any kind can become stressful; let alone after moving into a new house and throwing a party.

A Housewarming celebration, is designed to expand your social circle. Advise your clients that: with a stack of stationary cards to just go door to door and around the new neighbourhood.

In this case a time and date will be formally established and for all their neighbours, to show up announced; otherwise, they will be showing up unannounced, regardless. The event does not have to be formal as a wedding; however it might be similar to a wake and where people bring a lot of food platters.

It's really all up to the host and their family, to determine how formal or non-formal they would like their welcome home celebration. Housewarming parties usually tend to be on the more casual side. It is best to advise your clients, to simply take charge of the situation. It can become a wonderful opportunity for public speaking; so why not opt the over flimsy cue-cards, to create a meaningful script for them? Maybe the family might also prefer, the Celebrant as their Officiant. Otherwise the event, might involve the clients, to be tangled up and with various, unorganized distractions; such as, the sharing of gifts; saying a prayer and/or it can become more involved, with a ritual; or other traditional elements, to be explored with.

Depending on the celebration's theme and weather permitting; perhaps the ceremony can be held, out in the backyard and/or their condominium, recreation hall. Family and friends of your clients, can make it, even that much more, inviting and for others, who might not know them very well.

This can also include their realtor and home builders; as a final thank you for all their hard work.

The Family Celebrant & Officiant
Ceremony Theme & Culturally Combined Celebrations

Ask your client when and make certain to book within your timing comfort range for completion. Otherwise a reasonable explanation must be given to help the client understand; that the value and quality, might not be and as they would like to expect. This will better help resolve for any contingency and to further expand these ideas of a daytime socialization and/or a more formal night time dinner party? Then when they have grasped the moment back to feel more adventurous; ask about their preference on a theme? It can be anything, from an East Indian attire; to a Hawaiian dress code, with aloha shirts and light coloured pants; and/or revolve around the dining area, where all the food is placed on the table. Perhaps around a fireplace and where each guest can bring firewood. With that said, the pieces of charcoal from the first fire can help to start and/or can be picked up well after. Meaning that each guest who comes in offering firewood as a gift; can also be given some piece of charcoal to take with them. As a reminder, that they never feel the cold between their family and new found friends.

This gift can always be made to everyone and whilst holding onto the moments warmth; in their lives as a tribe and as a community. A fireplace symbolizes the hearth of the home and by warming up the hearts of those who gather. To experience this kind of warmth, can be a real heart opener and to those who can believe in how they resonate in better spirits. Some even go as far as to believe; that it creates a protective atmosphere of warmth. A pre entry Sanskrit ritual is commonly considered as a house warming, in Hindu cultures with a Pandit and before entering into a new house. Once that is done, there is nothing stopping the clients to have another more or less formal even as well. Where the first one is for the religious more intimate and private ceremony; where a Celebrant can be more looked upon to consider, is in the neighbourly meet and greet gathering.

Chapter Six
Ceremony Theme & Culturally Combined Celebrations

Aside from clearing/cleaning and removing evil spirits from a new flat. Celebrations and ceremony blessings are a great opportunity to decorate with flowers and/or for a certain dress code theme. A certain kind of "feng shui" can also be more prevalent amongst Asian cultures; where the sun, fire, water, earth and wind are energetically balanced. The ceremony can include to further emphasize these special areas; with a profound script, to imprint a blessing of prosperity and an easygoing flow. A non religious event and that can also care to include, the older members of the family; who might be more traditional, amidst chants and other mantras. The Celebrant can expand and to reinterpret, so to include all guests, be made to feel welcomed. What certain elements have and in their significance of where they are placed; such as, types of grains, spices and/or coins and even pots of milk, fruits and even coconuts. The vibes that all these decorations bring around the home and with their symbols to create perhaps a temple and why there. In this way all the neighbours, will become more encouraging; rather than become discouraged, every time they come to visit. Certain lamps can be lit and then placed in a salty water containment; incense, such as sandalwood too, can be lit. As well as other beautiful oil fragrances and pastes; that could otherwise enhance for this occasion. It is all about transmuting the energy field, within the home's surroundings; from a place of uneasiness, into a freer flowing and positively encouraging one, to our life force. Ultimately we all want to thrive and enjoy a blissfully peaceful life in a place that we can call our home. It is extremely important to take care of every small detail, so to avoid mistakes and to execute the entire ceremony in the right manner.

The Family Celebrant & Officiant
Chapter Seven ~ In Closing

Advertising & Having A Social Media Presence

Although cold calling might have worked before; ultimately going door-to-door, is a great way to feel a person out.
How they dress and present themselves. They might appear like an avatar online; but when face to face, haven't the kind of soulful and uplifting light to them(in real solid form); they might even smell bad. Do not dismiss the in person approach and in relation, to the many venues/ businesses; where the potential clients might frequent. This is a great opportunity to get a tour around the venue; to give out business cards and drop off some brochures and flyer. All the other formats, are done online and through Wireless Fidelity(WiFi). By creating your own website and purchasing a business domain name; this must be, your first priority. Then moving on, to Yelp, to advertise and makes for a great start; once an interaction has occurred, a charge is tallied. Other paid agencies can include: Wedding Wire, is highly competitive and very expensive, for Canadians; also it is more specific to a certain niche market. It can be great for Religious officials, just starting out and they do give many leads.
Event Source, is Canadian and designed for people who already have clients. When your business has grown and expanded from all the Yelp clients, then Event Source might be more useful. Again, it does not connect us to any potential customers and it is not recommended for those just starting out; be prepared, to also pay and for the entire year, up front. Every agency and website/domain has there own special offers make sure to shop around and sample as much as you can. So what might be the first option besides Yelp? Google Business, Linkedin, Twitter and Facebook/Instagram. Canadian Society Of Celebrants, is also providing a special link; a thread for its successful members, with a photo and a short biography.

Chapter Seven ~ In Closing
Society Vs. Association

What is the difference between a society and an association?

Although, Canadian Society Of Celebrants, does open its doors to everyone; it is a niche market and for Celebrants in Canada. Canadians(with exception to Quebec) and unlike our hybrid American neighbors, we as "neighbours", have several literary differences; that reflect academically, to "*honour*" and preserve, our British inherited English connotations. This is, a level of discernment, and one that can have us in the category of power, to choose by, as a consensus; rather than by the lack of inherited knowledge, to ignore(the wiping out, of yet another nation). What politically, might stand in its place, as incorrect; can dictate, the ruling from an uneducated and uninformed population. Associations have now become the new corporate American standard; a complete misnomer that has left the name society and with a very vague interpretation for any meaning to exist by it. The meaning of society has its backbone left in academia and certain other more disciplinary sanctions. Canadian Society Of Celebrants in this case, is somewhere in between the two; in that it does not involve as of yet, any legal restrictions, nor by-laws to adhere to, by its board members and committees alike. To categorize society in this way; it makes it very vague, in concept. From a business model perspective, it cares to benefit a niche social market, of people and that have the interest, as "Canadian Celebrants". This does not mean, that it will exclude, any other associations, to join in. The design, is to have an inner circle of un-reprimanded academic principles, set in place; through a scholarship level and for an initiation developed society. With that said, the value can be seen; from a level of expertise and that can respect the game enough, to build on these skills.

The Family Celebrant & Officiant

<u>Chapter Seven</u> ~ In Closing

Some Common Questions:

Is there a course I can take, where do I find it; how much does it cost and how can I start?

Maybe in the future, Canadian Society Of Celebrants might consider to modify and morph, as all the other associations and educational centres; however at this time, it is one of a kind, in Canada. You can't expect to leap, right into the course; because there are prerequisites to getting started. There are many people and places, who accept payment; whilst offering certification and diplomas and all you have to do, is show up for the entertainment. Why pay for large sums of money to be entertained and through social media accredited associated platforms; Or go to see professional guest speakers whilst paying for meals and rented staged venues. All these frills are entertainment and someone has to pay to help promote celebrity performances and public well known media, social influencers. What makes them better or any different from you?

The difference is, in the preference to invest this interest, to promote them; rather than yourselves. By letting someone else do all the work to entertain. Then at the end of the day a certificate, is granted and by the paid into accredited(for the permission, by those guest speakers) associations; to renew your many other licenses with and for putting in the time.

Canadian Society Of Celebrants, is not solely designed for that purpose. With that said and from reading volume one; it will not disclose this kind of apocalyptic revelation. It will take some time and for those with a real interest to come around.

You might have dismissed volume one and jumped right into this book; relax, that is alright too. What is not alright, is you not doing the work for yourselves and that is how we get results.

A bespoke course, can be provided to work on the weaknesses of each individual; through an assessment process. Without books, the result will be more intense, less effective and costing more.

Ceremony Guide   CSOC

The course, is a process designed by the Canadian Society Of Celebrants; this training intends to create strong and independent Celebrants. The main office, is located in Ontario; however, as the society continues to grow, so too, will the mentorship modifications and for its primary directives.
This will also likewise, reflect to better define our mission and visionary plans; for its future members and expanded collective membership. Furthermore, by working on our weaknesses, these books will help and with the clarity of assessment; for this reason and make for a wonderful prerequisite collection. This is the kind of awareness the curricula entails; for the readiness to hold down certain, for certification and as well to move on forth, onto obtaining a diploma. What makes this so very special, is that, it is not to impress others with(not so much the approval of others credits to ad value), no; this is all on you, the beholder of appreciation.
A reward is certain for every step of the way; that is offered to behold, whilst picking up the books and reading. The cost for the course begins with the purchase of a book. The only way that we can help is by the interest and the level of investment on yourself that you are willing to make. There are no shortcuts available at this time. With the purchase of the book we can help to advise so do not hesitate to reach out to us.
canadiansocietyofcelebrantss@gmail.com

This is a learning process, created to enable the experience; through its expanded perception and from your leverage of belief, within your capabilities. To stretch your imagination, into giving the permission it deserves; to help the world, at large and with what it thinks, it can or cannot do. The cost starts with the purchase of Volume One. The idea of, a one on one tutorial and assignments comes in after. These planned payments, will be further discussed and broken down each tier; with an à la carte flexible component and a step by step prerequisite process.

The Family Celebrant & Officiant
Chapter Seven ~ In Closing

The Questionnaire:

Q.1. Have you considered by now, what your pricelist might look like?
Create a menu and from it, pick for the following next question.

You have your very first client interested in your services.
Give a complete break down from start to finish and on how to go about creating a ceremony?

Q.2. Describe the Ceremony Script comprised components (the order of service), from start to finish and how the Anatomy would look?

Q.3. What is your take away from this format and how could you improve on the many samples from your experience?

Is the system helping you to expand on your horizon?

Q.4. Just how has it helped to better inform and educate your future clients; on the value that a Ceremony does and can provide?

Q.5. Explain the significance of having an imagination; how would you go about sharing this importance, with your clients?

The Questionnaire:

How long does it take to go through the course?

What are the prerequisites and for each step; how can I go about getting a diploma?

Lastly, is there more than one course offered for certification?

It really is not about the how much money the student can save; rather the more practiced, the more credibility is warranted and can reflect, much more accurately for any approval.
Canadian Society Of Celebrants, is designed for the leader in you and not for the weak and meek at heart; doubt is not in our thoughts to encourage.

When you finally reach at this level of knowing, it is time, to go out there and spread the word.... You got this!

The Family Celebrant & Officiant

Chapter 8 : WHERE DO WE GO FROM HERE ?

Have you completed "Volume One" and already received the Funeral Celebrant certification?
This is where Phase 2: The Advanced package can be handy; rather than having to take the "Intermediate Learners" package (however these options are available). You have successfully made it through this book's reading achievement.
Welcome to the next stage of the process; to gain certification and/or skip right up, to a diploma.

Step 1: email the following to,
canadiansocietyofcelebrantss@gmail.com
Your name as you prefer to have it show on the certification and your place of residence address for proper mailing of an authenticated sealed and approved by the CSOC.
Please include a telephone contact number; email and/or other video live chat connections. Upon request: further training and tutoring package of preference. "The Intermediate Learners" package, is Phase (1)&(2); or "The Advanced" package, Phase(2). The Intermediate package; to conclude with(Upon receipt of payment) the following developments, toward a successful Family Celebrant Certification:
Phase (1) A course handout to include, an Interview Checklist, of a mock scenario and from it; the following documents:
(a) A Celebrant Ceremony Draft + an Anatomy Of Ceremony.
(b) A Client Ceremony Script.
(c) A video of your rehearsal(as you would present it).
  Appointments can be adjusted, for one on one, live grading and assistance with tutor(to play the others part in script). Interactive communications can take place, to answer any questions and exactly as it would be; when dealing with in real time and with clients(by calling them up to ask for any missing information).

Ceremony Guide   CSOC

WHERE DO WE GO FROM HERE ?

"The Advanced" package: will conclude with the following developments, to a successful Family Celebrant Certification:

Phase (2) A booking with a client for a ceremony.
  After making contact with your client, the following considerations must be made:

(a) A copy of (after all revisions have been made) "The Celebrant Ceremony Script" and attached to it, with "The Anatomy Of a Ceremony".

(b) A Copy as you would be giving to your client of "The Client Ceremony Script".

(c) Prior to the actual ceremony; a video copy of a well rehearsed ceremony.

(d) As soon as a booking is to take place and without any delay; (ASAP) contact us to VIP in a mentor.

To finalize a grade of accomplishment; distinctly sign your book and as you too, will witness. "Volume Two" will become, your very own reference, at hand and you will be well on your way; to the next "stage of the process"(if you so wish it), as a Funeral Celebrant with Volume 1. (Volume 1 + Volume 2 = Diploma).

(e) You are to make a photo copy of the "Practical Evaluation and Examination Sheet".
Along with (a)+(b)+(c) submit to us for your final grade And hurray, your certification will be on its way.

***NOTE**: Further instructions and cost brake down; will be made readily available, in the online handouts.

The Family Celebrant & Officiant
Practical Evaluation and Examination Sheet:

(Include what day) Date: _____ Time Start ____ : ____ Finish ____ : ____

Name of Mentor _____ Sign _____

Name of Venue _____

Name of Student _____ Sign _____

CEREMONY TYPE: _____

TOTAL GRADE OF PERFORMANCE   CS✫C

_____

Public Speaking: _____ /25%
Voice Conduct   /10% Connection   /10% Confidence   /5%

Officiating: _____ /25%
Synergy   /6% Synchronicity   /6% Leadership   /13%

Content of Script: _____ /30%
Synergy   /10% Synchronicity   /10% Depth/Quality   /10%

Appearance: _____ /20%
Image Conduct   /10%   Self Esteem   /10%

canadiansocietyofcelebrantss@gmail.com

www.ingramcontent.com/pod-product-compliance
Lightning Source LLC
Chambersburg PA
CBHW051705160426
43209CB00004B/1023